Know Your Place

'I still remember that day in March 1968 when our Lisbon Lions team visited Martin Naughton and the other children in the institution in Baldoyle. The impression we got was that these kids had been forgotten, abandoned by society. It left a mark on us all and I often thought about them when I looked at my own children.'

John Fallon, Glasgow Celtic European Cup-winning team of 1967

'Martin was a formidable and tireless campaigner for the right of people with disabilities to live in their own communities and homes.'

President Michael D Higgins

"Martin Naughton was a protector, a leader, a gamechanger. In reading this narration of his life, tears filled my eyes.'

    Dr Rosaleen McDonagh, playwright, rights activist, author of *Unsettled*

'Martin Naughton was a leader not only in Ireland, but in Europe and the United States. His personal experiences with his disability enabled him to understand not only the plight of disabled people but also how critical it was to encourage people to have a vision for what their life could be.'

    Judy Heumann, US activist, author of
Being Heumann: An Unrepentant Memoir of a Disability Rights Activist

'I had the privilege of standing with Martin Naughton on a number of campaigns and projects. He was an inspiring activist, a courageous and mighty warrior.'

Christy Moore, singer and songwriter

'I was waiting in the lobby of the Royal Dublin Hotel when the door was pushed open for a man in a wheelchair, wearing a fishing hat, with a cigarette sticking out of his mouth. He brought me into the CIL office on Bolton Street, where I was astonished to encounter a group of militant wheelchair-users passionately committed to changing the world. This was in sharp contrast to the perception of disability I had been brought up with – people who were passive, dependent and objects of pity and charity.'

Christian O'Reilly, writer of *Sanctuary*, *Inside I'm Dancing* and *No Magic Pill* (a stage play inspired by the life of Martin Naughton)

'If the Independent Living movement was a mafia, Martin would have been our Don; he was always trying to think of new and seemingly radical ways of equalising the playing field …. Now that he has passed from this world, we have to ensure that his legacy lives on.'

Sarah Fitzgerald, activist and writer of *Conversations About Activism and Change*

'*Never Know Your Place* brilliantly recounts disabled people's resistance to segregation. Martin's life and activism will resonate deeply with so many – from survivors of mother and baby homes to those still living in direct provision – charting the path from institutionalisation to freedom.'

Eilionóir Flynn, Director, Centre for Disability Law and Policy, University of Galway

'Martin was a gentleman. We connected on the level that those with indigenous drive do. I was involved in the founding of the Center for Independent Living and met great people on that road. We are all institutionalised one way or another, and it is our duty to listen to those who broke through with truth and energy to reveal our right to freedom as human beings. Martin's voice speaks for the human soul.'

Liam Ó Maonlaí, musician

'A compelling story of a man who was determined to have his say in the world, and also a reminder that activism is not just about big campaigns, it's about the small everyday ways we change the world around us for the better.'

James Cawley, disabled activist

MARTIN NAUGHTON (1954–2016) was a disabled activist from Spiddal, County Galway, who lived most of his life in Baldoyle in north Dublin. Having experienced institutionalisation and fought hard for his freedom, he became a life-long advocate for the right of disabled people to live independently. Through his personal friendships with American activists, he was instrumental in spreading the Independent Living movement to Ireland, and in the mid-1990s he led the landmark political campaign for Personal Assistant services. His later achievements include founding the 'ENIL Freedom Drive', a biennial event which brings disabled people from Europe together in Brussels to highlight the right to Independent Living.

JOANNA MARSDEN is a writer and independent radio documentary-maker who grew up in England and Ireland and now lives in Dún Laoghaire. She has written for publications including *The Irish Times* and got to know Martin when she interviewed him for a book about how life had changed for disabled people in Ireland. Her projects include making documentaries for Newstalk and RTÉ Lyric FM, and contributing to TULCA Festival of Visual Arts.

Martin Naughton

With Joanna Marsden

Never Know Your Place

MEMOIR OF A RULEBREAKER

With a foreword by Dr Rosaleen McDonagh
And an afterword by Niall Ó Baoill

THE O'BRIEN PRESS
DUBLIN

First published 2024 by The O'Brien Press Ltd,
12 Terenure Road East, Rathgar, Dublin 6, D06 HD27, Ireland.
Tel: +353 1 4923333; Fax: +353 1 4922777
E-mail: books@obrien.ie. Website: obrien.ie
The O'Brien Press is a member of Publishing Ireland.

ISBN: 978-1-78849-452-6

Text © Joanna Marsden 2024
The moral rights of the author have been asserted.
Editing, typesetting, layout, design © The O'Brien Press Ltd
Cover and inside design by Emma Byrne.

All rights reserved. No part of this publication may be reproduced or utilised in any form or by any means, electronic or mechanical, including for text and data mining, training artificial intelligence systems, photocopying, recording or in any information storage and retrieval system, without permission in writing from the publisher.

8 7 6 5 4 3 2 1
28 27 26 25 24

The author and publisher thank the following for permission to use photographs and illustrative material:
Photographs: pp. 22, 33, 34, 37, 61, 64, 84, 92, 94, 104, 117, 135, 148, 174 are reproduced with kind permission of Barbara Naughton, the Naughton family and Niall Ó Baoill. Others are courtesy of: p. 44 (photograph by James G Maguire) and p. 26 (bottom right), both Abbey Theatre Archive; pp. 56, 95 Teresa Byrne; p.63 sourced from CelticWiki; p. 189 Michael Dawson; pp. 79, 102, 103, 108, 121, 123 John Duffy; pp. 190 Mary Duffy; p. 70 Kathleen Reynolds; p. 156 Bruce Fay and Trish Irons; p. 159 Judy Heumann/Kelila Weiner; pp. 28, 51, 55 Michael J Hurley Collection; pp. 164, 171 (top), 173 (both) ILMI; pp. 27, 58 Lensmen/Irish Photo Archive; p. 167 Irish Wheelchair Association; p. 25 photograph © George R Mahony and p. 26 (bottom left) photograph © Kevin A Murray, both courtesy Ciarán Cooney, IRRS Archive; p. 128 Mary Llewellyn; pp. 138, 150, 153 Robby Martin; pp. 186, 187 Áiseanna Tacaíochta; p. 89 sourced from National Paralympic Heritage Trust UK; p. 171 (bottom both) Marc O'Sullivan; p. 85 Dermot Ring.

Front cover photograph: Dermot Ring.

If any involuntary infringement of copyright has occurred, sincere apologies are offered, and the owners of such copyright are requested to contact the publisher.

Printed and bound by CPI Group (UK) Ltd, Croydon, CR0 4YY.
The paper in this book is produced using pulp from managed forests.

Published in

Dedication

To my loving family, who always encouraged me to think big.
To the people who inspired me and kept me going through
the tough years in Baldoyle Hospital, and the friends who later
supported me and took joy in my independence.
To all my PAs, without whom it would have been impossible to live
such a rich and free life.
To the other disabled people who fought for change alongside me,
many of whom are no longer with us.

Tá buíochas mór ag dul do mo thuismitheoirí agus do mo mhuintir
as ucht na tacaíochta, na comhairle agus an spreagtha a thug siad
dom chun mo dhícheall a dhéanamh i gcónaí.
Buíochas mór dóibh siúd ar fad a thug cúnamh dom ar bhealach
amháin nó ar bhealach eile, go mórmhór m'fhoireann tacaíochta,
chun ceann scríbe a bhaint amach.
Dóibh siúd, cosúil liom féin, a sheas liom agus a thug a gcroíthe agus
a n-anamacha le saol níos fearr a bhaint amach.
Go raibh maith agaibh!

Martin Naughton

Contents

My Time with Martin by Joanna Marsden	page 13
Foreword by Dr Rosaleen McDonagh	18
Prologue	22
1: Day One	24
2: Thirteen Acres of Rock	31
3: Other People's Rules	39
4: The Batmobile	49
5: Bottom of the Heap	53
6: Listening to the Lions	60
7: Daring to Dream	69
8: Head above Water	76
9: From Patient to Taxpayer	82
10: Something about Mary	93
11: Baldoyle Boys	99
12: Special Treatment	107
13: Bringing Home the Bacon	114
14: The Real World	120
15: The Hat	127
16: Dreams and Regrets	131
17: Independent State of Mind	139

18: Throwing out the Rule Book	144
19: Know your Story	152
20: Operation Get-Out	163
Epilogue	177
Afterword by Niall Ó Baoill	182
Co-author's Notes	191
Endnotes	195
Acknowledgements	199

My Time with Martin

Joanna Marsden

Martin Naughton had a way of letting everyone know he was in a room. A dramatic hat (in his older years a flat skullcap, in earlier decades a tweed cap or a fedora), wispy long hair and a goatee. Before I knew him, I'd seen him once or twice at events and noticed a bit of fuss as he arrived, his visible impatience when he disagreed with what someone was saying, and how as he made his way around the room with his Personal Assistant alongside, he would give a firm nod to anyone he knew or was interested in knowing.

I didn't know the younger Martin whose story is told in this memoir. The first time I met Martin properly was in 2010 when I interviewed him for a book on how life had changed for disabled people in Ireland.

'Glad something is being written,' he said. 'The histories of marginalised people are too often forgotten.'

His final comment in that first interview was pointed: 'The credit for what has been achieved so far belongs to no organisation, it belongs to disabled people themselves.'

A few years later, I got an email from him saying he needed to talk to me about a piece of work.

Never Know Your Place

'I'll meet you on your turf,' he said.

Later that week, at the Marine Hotel in Dún Laoghaire, he explained he wanted to leave a written account of his life and of the political battle to free disabled people from institutions and get funding for Personal Assistant (PA) services. He was sixty and with a progressive disability like his he said, 'It should have been lights out long ago.'

He didn't know how much longer his luck would last.

The memoir was first and foremost about setting the record straight, making sure the events he'd lived through were not forgotten.

'If people forget, it's easier to go backwards,' he said, alluding to the fact that budgets for PA hours were always under threat. 'Even if this just ends up a pile of paper and photos in a corner of the Centre for Disability Law and Policy in Galway, it's worth writing.'

I understood. 'You know if you put the word "disability" into the National Library's digital photographic archive, you get one photo of a woman with an orthopaedic shoe,' I told him, this being something I had discovered the week before.

He raised his eyebrows. 'When we're done with this, let's put that right.'

Over the subsequent two years, Martin and I met every couple of months at his terraced cottage in Baldoyle village to work on the book.

Early on, when he spoke about his childhood and first years in Baldoyle Hospital, his memories came forcefully, as if locked in his heart for too long.

'I had a rough night after that last session,' he admitted one morning.

But as he grew older in the narrative, what I came to think of as the 'political' Martin emerged. He could talk forever about the steps in his journey to independence and the development of his political thinking, but

My Time with Martin

he found it hard to talk directly about his emotional life.

'I want to be open. I want to tell you everything we need to write this,' he told me, 'but I'm used to keeping my cards close to my chest.'

Seeing him sometimes visibly frustrated as he tried to find the words made me wonder about the consequences of being torn away at the age of nine from his native language and having to learn English in a medical institution. I also thought about how hard it must have been for Martin to protect his privacy in that institution and even after he moved to his own home because of his requirement for twenty-four-hour PA support.

Co-writing a story is a strange process, because you find yourself needing to read between the lines in the conversations that take place. If you come from a different background, as I do as a non-disabled female writer who grew up over two decades later, this isn't always easy. I remember questioning, for example, why Martin wanted to talk so much about the character of 'JC', the quintessential Haughey-era businessman who gave him his first job outside the hospital. It took a conversation with Rosaleen McDonagh to remind me that not only was it incredibly rare for a man with a disability like Martin's to get a job in the private sector, but such a job was also symbolic of a type of patriarchal power that would have felt unattainable to a disabled boy growing up in 1960s Ireland.

I often heard Martin referred to as 'the father of the Irish Independent Living movement' and, in the best of ways, I think this was true. It's also notable that many of the men in Martin's early life followed a pattern: they were traditional providers, and yet they were also nurturing characters, who looked out for the young people around them and deferred to the women in their households.

Perhaps because of my own perspective, I was drawn straightaway to the women in Martin's early life, such as his mother Nora and his older sister Maureen. They seemed unpredictable and formidable characters. Sometimes, as with the senior nun he called the 'White Tornado', they were the rulemakers. But their lives felt curtailed. They were surviving in a society with few options, and I was struck by the empathy Martin had for that.

When Martin died in October 2016, this book was a draft. I eventually completed it by drawing on notes and recordings, and by talking to Martin's sister Barbara and his close friends. A list of those who contributed can be found in the Acknowledgements, but particular thanks is owed to Niall Ó Baoill, Rosaleen McDonagh, Hubert McCormack (RIP), Kathleen Reynolds, Mary Llewellyn, and Gordana Rajkov (RIP), each of whom shared memories and anecdotes, and to Allen Dunne (DFI), Selina Bonnie (ILMI), Michael Doyle (IWA) and Michael Dawson, who helped bring the project to completion.

At its heart this is a memoir of boyhood and the making of the political animal that was Martin Naughton. The book ends in 1995 with the political campaign for PA funding that Martin considered his greatest achievement. If you are curious about the final two decades of Martin's life, in which there were significant achievements, you will find some information in Niall Ó Baoill's Afterword.

Today we take it for granted that disabled people are a visible part of our communities. We think nothing when we pass a wheelchair user in the street, and we don't notice if that wheelchair user has a PA beside them. But this book may remind you that there was a time, not that long ago, when things were different. If you were around in that time, you may find yourself asking, why did I not notice that disabled people were not there?

Martin would have been happy to think of you reading his story. It was not an easy story for him to tell, but he went to great lengths to tell it because he feared that in history, as in politics, 'If it's not in writing, it never happened.' It is in this spirit that half the royalties of the book will go into a fund in Martin's name, which will begin by devising three small bursaries with the Irish Writers Centre to encourage other disabled people to tell their stories.

Foreword

Dr Rosaleen McDonagh

Martin Naughton was a constant figure in my life. Almost a surrogate father. In reading this narration of his life, tears filled my eyes. The memories are not just wrapped up in a sense of nostalgia, they hold a picture of a man who was a protector, a leader, a gamechanger. The book is also personal to me in that many of Martin's peers within the disability movement, who organised so much disabled activism, have now also passed. It would be naïve to suggest that Martin and his peers only planted seeds. They did a lot more than that. They managed to change social policy in relation to people with disability in Ireland.

The difficulty with producing this book is that Martin passed before the manuscript was completed. Even in death, this man managed to remain somewhat elusive. The suggestion that he would trust the writer Joanna Marsden to carry out his wishes by documenting his experience gives us a glimpse of what Martin saw as his role. He was an ideas man. The rest of us had to chisel and nail those ideas into something practical and functional. Martin was complex, often closed off emotionally, warm but not always free. He was a private man with a public persona. My admiration goes to Joanna who had to work on notes and conversations with Martin, and who

Foreword

essentially had to do a lot of her own research.

The book is a tribute not just to Martin but to people around him, the work they've done and the accessible paths through education and independent living that were created because of Martin's leadership and vision. The book itself is innovative in that it documents the growth of the disability movement here in Ireland and worldwide. It's also, and probably more importantly, a definite celebration of disabled lives.

Martin continuously attempted to move out of a place that was designated to him. That place was segregated, held only for the poor, the disabled. Martin, who lived his life during six decades of great change in Ireland, absolutely believed that designated space was too small for him. He recognised from an early age that he and those around him did not live in a vacuum. He used that segregated space as a platform to build the political consciousness of five generations of Irish disabled people. While he abhorred exclusion and discrimination resulting in low expectations and lack of citizenship, Martin managed to build momentum within that segregated area, so that the struggle for change became a collective journey.

From Connemara to Dublin, from Dublin to Boston, DC and Berkeley, and then in his final year on to Montgomery, Alabama, Martin's nomadic spirit was very much influenced by Connemara culture as well as Irish culture. He wanted to spread the fire of the American Civil Rights and Independent Living Movements and capture the spirit and the energy of the anti-racist movement, bringing that drive into the disability movement and disability politics.

In his later years, Martin reengaged with music, and nostalgia for the Miami Showband was one of his few pleasures. He was a busy man, a man that had things to do, a man with a huge memory and an ever-expanding

Never Know Your Place

heart full of generosity. He was a player. He knew politics, be it big, small or partisan. He could work a room. His charisma surpassed your average charmer.

For me, there are no early memories or first memories of Martin. He was just there. He was in charge, a man that would get things done. A man that fooled us all into believing that Baldoyle Hospital Sports Club with its disabled athletes was about winning medals. It wasn't. The Sports Club was not only about showcasing talent, but it was also about integration, about getting young people from the local area to come into the segregated hospital environment so young people with and without disabilities could mix. Martin saw the value in these symbolic friendships across divides. If we, the residents of Baldoyle Hospital, could not access the world, then the outside world could be brought in to us.

Martin saw potential not just in the winners but in people like me, those of us who were mediocre. Those of us that were often quickly written off or erased. Many of us were lucky enough to sit around and listen to him while he told us stories of what was happening in Berkeley, California during the eighties and nineties. He managed to convince us that if Independent Living could happen over there, it could also happen here in Ireland. He was the first man I knew who had his own accessible transport; the first man I knew who managed to live in his own house. He galvanised a group of people like me to start to demand higher expectations for ourselves. That higher expectation was built on a strong collective self-esteem which poked and prodded service providers to do what hadn't been done before. For many of us when we got in trouble Martin was the one that we would call. That trouble, regardless of the magnitude, was very often not understood by a non-disabled person. Rights and self-determination: this was the language he gave us.

Foreword

Martin also paid for my confirmation outfit. He paid for the hotel where I celebrated with my family after I got my degree. In those days it wasn't just about money, it was about Travellers knowing a settled person and being able to use a settled person's name to gain access.

Martin spoke beautiful Irish. In the middle of a conversation, he would sporadically use sentences and words, almost forgetting the present moment and briefly running back to Connemara, if not physically most definitely spiritually and linguistically. He was a passionate man, a man that could easily make you cry. A man that would notice when you went off the radar. He would send someone to find you.

In the months before Martin died in October 2016 he had buried a number of his fellow Center for Independent Living members and founders. Together these founders were known as 'The Magnificent Seven'. The fragility of life and fragility of disabled bodies were ever present in those three years before Martin passed. For many of us, we were still living our dream. For some, this meant having received a service package for Personal Assistance hours, for others it was about being able to buy their own accessible vehicle or being able to use accessible public transport. He had built a movement, a concept, a message, a philosophy, a legacy that younger disabled people have inherited without questioning its origins.

Martin died just weeks after going into hospital in late August 2016. Those of us who he left behind were worried about our social and cultural influence without our great leader. Many of us were angry. He left no instructions or no warning. It took me a while to realise that was Martin. He absolutely believed young people would reshape and rejuvenate the Independent Living Movement in Ireland. His last words to me were, 'Make room for strangers and keep our fire lit.'

Prologue

Martin and Barbara in their first year at St Mary's Orthopaedic Hospital for Children in Baldoyle. Probably taken in spring/summer 1964 when Martin was nine or ten, and Barbara seven or eight. Martin had begun using a wheelchair most of the time but transferred to the bench for the photo.

I have never blamed my parents for sending my sister Barbara and me away from our family home in the Irish-speaking seaside village of Spiddal in County Galway to St Mary's Orthopaedic Hospital for

Prologue

Children in Baldoyle, Dublin. Powerful religious orders funded residential institutions for children with physical disabilities like us, but neither they nor the State offered any practical, therapeutic or financial support to parents who kept their disabled children at home. No one spoke to any parent and said, 'What services do you need?' No one said, 'Well, there's this and that available.' Huge institutions like St Mary's *were* Ireland's Welfare State.

In 1963, the year the decision to send us to St Mary's was made, my mother was fifty years old. Her skin was a little rosy, but she had high cheekbones and a certain fineness to her. She wore her greying brown hair in a loose bun, and when at home, had a neat floral apron tied around her waist. She had given birth to ten children, and though still sprightly enough, I think our new local doctor, who was a bright young woman with something of a feminist perspective, may well have looked at her and asked, 'Is it right that this woman, who has already raised a big family, should surrender the rest of her life to being a full-time carer for two young disabled people?'

In later years, I think everyone in the family wondered whether a mistake had been made, but I reminded them that it is society – and the supports it does or does not offer to families – that really makes these decisions. What choice did my parents, and hundreds of others like them, really have?

Chapter 1

Day One

I was nine years old when the day came for my younger sister Barbara and me to leave Spiddal. It was 4 October 1963. That Friday morning the Galway bus, which passed through the village once a day, came by arrangement to the door of the bungalow my father had just finished building. My father handed our small suitcase to the driver and lifted Barbara and me over the metal step. As I made my way towards my seat, holding onto the back of each chair as I passed, it was the last time he would see me walking.

One of our older sisters, Mairéad, had been given the job of accompanying us the whole way to Baldoyle in Dublin, where the Sisters at St Mary's Orthopaedic Hospital for Children were expecting us. Mairéad was only seventeen, but she spoke decent English and had a good helping of common sense.

In Galway, Mairéad got the three of us safely onto the Dublin train, where we sat beside a family with children who offered to let us share their toys. Barbara pushed Dinky cars up and down the aisle on her knees, but I stayed in my seat by the window, propping my shoulder against the frame to hold myself upright. I watched the unfamiliar faces get on and off at each station. Though I had taken the train to Athenry a few times, I had never travelled this far.

Day One

The Phoenix Park Tunnel as captured from an approaching train on the Kingsbridge side of the tunnel, c. 1959.

As we approached Dublin, the train entered a tunnel. It was the first time I'd been in a tunnel, and the way the lights flashed on seconds after the darkness engulfed us was thrilling. In the years afterwards, I often wondered if I had imagined this tunnel, because I never travelled through it again, and it seemed so dramatic in my memory – as if it marked the moment we passed from one world into another.

The train came to a halt at Westland Row Station. Our parents had given strict instructions that we were to wait in our carriage until Mícheál Ó Bríain, one of our neighbours from Spiddal who was living in Dublin, came to collect us.[1] The three of us sat there as the minutes passed. We started to think he wasn't coming. One of the station staff stepped on board and tried to encourage us to disembark, but Mairéad insisted we had to wait for Mícheál.

The train's engines started again as the driver readied it for the journey to its next destination – the ferry terminal in Dún Laoghaire, I think – and

Never Know Your Place

just in time Micheál stepped onto the carriage and swept us off. I felt a rush of excitement as we entered the vast station building. Micheál Ó Bríain, or Mickeen as he was known to us, worked as a 'resident' actor in the Abbey Theatre and he must have been a well-known face in Dublin, because passers-by greeted him enthusiastically.

He led the three of us out of the station into the damp afternoon and at our slow pace we made our way past rows of tall houses and shops with unfamiliar names until we reached the swollen Liffey and crossed to a bus stop on the quays.

Like most people, Barbara and I knew our destination only as the 'Little Willie', after the boy who appeared in newspaper adverts as the mascot of the hospital's fundraising campaigns. Little Willie wore callipers to help him stand and the slogan beside him said, 'Help Little Willie who cannot help himself'.

Bottom left: The interior of Westland Row Station (now Pearse Street Station), where Martin, Barbara and Mairéad arrived and were met by Micheál Ó Bríain. Photograph 1967.

Bottom right: Spiddal native Micheál Ó Bríain. This photograph of Micheál was used in the Abbey Theatre programmes in the 1960s.

Day One

'Little Willie', the young boy who featured in hospital fundraising campaigns, is pictured here (wearing callipers) with an unidentified girl and comedy legends Stan Laurel and Oliver Hardy. The occasion is the presentation of a cheque on behalf of Premier (DOMAS) to the Little Willie Fund in September 1953.

The Number 32 bus was a double-decker, but we sat on the lower floor close to the driver, Mícheál and I sharing one seat, and Mairéad and Barbara sharing the one behind. As we travelled northwards out of the city, I looked out the steamed-up window at the grey buildings and thought how enormous everything was and how the roads in Dublin went on forever.

'That way to Croke Park,' Mícheál said, pointing left.

'This is Annesley Bridge,' he said. 'We're coming into Fairview now.'

I'd not been to a capital city before. Galway was the only city I'd seen. I thought how I'd better shape up if I was going to take care of Barbara and

Never Know Your Place

myself in this unfamiliar place.

'Where's the "Little Willie", Micheál?' I asked in Irish.

'I've not been there, Martin, but don't you worry, we are on the right bus.'

I found it strange that Micheál could not tell us exactly where the hospital was since it was clear he knew the rest of Dublin like the back of his hand.

It felt like hours, but when I saw grey flat-roofed blocks looming behind the small, terraced cottages of Baldoyle Village and the driver gave Micheál a nod, I wondered how anybody in Dublin, let alone Micheál, could not know where the Little Willie was.

St Mary's Orthopaedic Hospital for Children, as the Little Willie was officially called, was a sprawling complex, with the hospital part at the south

An aerial photo of Baldoyle in 1962, as taken for an 'Aeroviews' postcard, showing the recently built St Mary's Orthopaedic Hospital for Children in Baldoyle.

Day One

end and the Convent of the Sisters of Charity at the north end, close to the village bus stop. The four of us wandered in through the convent door, which had been left ajar by a lady with a mop and bucket. Micheál left us on a bench in the hall while he went ahead to introduce himself.

He returned minutes later, having been chastised by one of the Sisters.

'They're giving out because we've come in the wrong door,' he said.

Taking a quick look behind him, he puffed up his chest and stuck his chin in the air to mimic the Sister, *'That door, Mr Ó Bríain, is strictly out of bounds to patients.'*[2]

Micheál must have been a smooth talker though because the Sister arrived a minute later and told us she had decided to make an exception. She led us through the long corridors of the convent towards the hospital building. I was coming to the natural end of my walking life, and the more tired my legs were, the less they did what my brain asked of them. Micheál saw this and he passed the suitcase to Mairéad and scooped me up. Barbara, who was steadier on her feet than me, walked behind us. I wouldn't see that part of the building again for many years, but in those first minutes, even though I was in Micheál's strong arms, the echoing corridors of the convent gave me the creeps.

Once Micheál and Mairéad had left, Barbara and I were immediately separated and absorbed into the hospital system.

First I was sent to confession. When the priest heard my pidgin English, he said, 'Don't worry, Martin. God speaks many languages.'

'See you next week with a brand-new show!' I said as I left the confession box and he laughed. That's a phrase I'd learned from Radio Luxembourg and it was one of my favourite English expressions.

After confession I was given a haircut by the hospital porter, Kit Byrne.

Never Know Your Place

'You can call me Kit,' he said with an informality that seemed at odds with the rest of the place.

Kit was a wiry man of about thirty, whose dark fringe was greased back by a spicy smelling cream that I inhaled as he leaned in. He tried to show me a little kindness, chatting as he worked, but I hated haircuts. I was then sent to have a bath, despite my protestations that my parents had given me one only the night before (in those days baths were supposed to be a weekly chore).

Only when clean in body and spirit could I be presented to the hospital doctor for a full medical inspection. I had been afraid to ask to use the toilet all day, and it was late in the afternoon by the time I reached the doctor's office. One prod of my distended tummy and I was sent straight back out.

That first day at Baldoyle Hospital, as we would soon come to call it, was very difficult. I had to be brave because there was no one to cry to. Looking back, I realise that the confession, the haircut, the bath, the medical – these were all just elements of a routine Friday, rather than a special initiation process for arrivals like Barbara and me. The institution followed a strict routine each day, with no allowance for the feelings of new children unused to this regimented way of life. And when it came to that first night, I felt the terrible feeling I was often to experience in the months that followed. Lying in my metal bed in the boys' ward, listening to the unfamiliar sounds of echoing steps in corridors and hushed staff voices, I cried for home, for myself, for Barbara.

Chapter 2

Thirteen Acres of Rock

I was born on 16 March 1954 in the same thatched stone cottage in which my father, Peadar Ó Neachtain, had been born forty-four years earlier. My father had taken over the small family farm when his elder brothers had left for Boston to work on the railroads. The farm was a couple of miles east of Spiddal village and had a fine view of Galway Bay.

'I have the privilege of owning thirteen acres of rock,' he used to joke.

Although he farmed the land as intensively as he could, it only produced the equivalent of a good allotment. But my father was a natural salesman and he went to market regularly, where he sold turf, vegetables, and carrageen seaweed, as well as some cattle and sheep. He supplemented his farming income by working as a horseman, offering haulage services and taxiing spectators at the Galway races each year in his cart.

My mother, Nora Feeney, had grown up in North Spiddal, just a few miles from my father. They had known each other all their lives and she was twenty-three when they married in 1936, and forty-two by the time she had me, the second youngest of her ten children. Two of her six siblings had gone to Boston, but the rest remained in Spiddal. She was inseparable from two of her sisters, who would spend much of each day in our house. It must have been accepted that my mother couldn't go to their houses

Never Know Your Place

because, though we'd many cousins, Barbara and I needed the most minding. My aunts would sit around the open fire in the main room of our cottage, while my mother cooked and cleaned. During the day, the stable-style front door would be half open, to keep the chickens out while my mother kept an eye on us playing outside, and in the evenings I was sometimes allowed to curl up on my mother's lap beside the fire as they chatted into the night. Their conversations were an endless source of entertainment for me, and from early on I formed the impression that my mother came from a family of strong, clever women, with a great sixth sense. I listened as they spoke about the people they had come across – be it in the village shop or at church – and I noticed how they never took anyone at face value, but rather considered what motivated them. They seemed to have an intuitive understanding of how the world worked despite rarely having moved far beyond their garden gates.

My eldest sister Maureen was sixteen by the time I was born and was like a second mother to me. Maureen had been diagnosed with muscular dystrophy as a young child and thus had brought my parents their first experience of disability. As a young woman, she walked with difficulty, but nonetheless she had beauty and exuded confidence. She made sure she joined in with every activity at home or in Spiddal village, including having the odd *deoch* in the local pub, even when others implied she had no right to because of her disability or her gender. She was also well read, in a time when the only ordinary women to have a good standard of education were those in religious orders, and this had earned the respect of both my parents. People in the village would often ask Maureen to help them write letters to relatives in America or book one-way tickets to America for themselves. Maureen was full of dreams, and she talked about going to

Martin's father, Peadar Ó Neachtain, on the small family farm, which was a couple of miles east of Spiddal village.

America herself one day. It seemed to me that all the time she was working against the odds and looking to the future.

In those early years, Maureen influenced me more than anyone else. In fact, when my parents first spotted my odd way of standing and the way I kept falling, they thought I was copying her. It must have been a disappointment when they realised I shared her disability. At the same time, Maureen was such a positive example of how to live with a disability. Knowing Maureen could hold her own in the world was certainly

Never Know Your Place

Martin's mother, Nora Feeney, who had grown up in North Spiddal, just a few miles from where she settled when she married Peadar Ó Neachtain.

important for my father, and it made it easier for him to accept my condition. I think my mother would have liked it if I'd had more physical perfection, but that wouldn't just have been about walking right.

Maureen was one of six elder siblings. The second eldest was Bridgie, known to us by her middle name Chris. My earliest memory is of seventeen-year-old Chris leaving for America when I was about four years old. It was a hugely sad day, but thereafter our life was punctuated by the excitement of regular letters (the letters meant a lot – the few bob inside even more). I remember the joy of Chris coming home for a summer holiday a couple of years later, dressed like Jackie Onassis.

Below Chris was my brother Pádraic, then Mairéad (also known sometimes as Peig), Cait and Bernie.

Maureen and I – and Barbara, who arrived on the scene a year after me – were the only ones to develop a disability, but my parents had also lost two children before I was born. Their first child, Nóirín, had died of tuberculosis when she was eleven, and their third child, Séamus, had died of whooping cough when he was two. Having looked both disability and death in the face, they didn't court worry or drama. They had seen so many ups and downs by the time Barbara and I were diagnosed that the only urgency was to do the best they could that day. They believed if they kept doing that, all would be well in the end.

At seven years of age, I began attending the local national school in Spiddal, where I spent two years before leaving for Baldoyle. The lads at the school fell into two rival groups: lads from the village and lads from the areas outside the village. I was an exception in that I got on with both groups. Although our house was just outside the village, my closest friends were village boys, and despite my disability, I was never picked upon. There

Never Know Your Place

seemed to be an understanding that I wasn't going to be touched. It helped that my best friend was Seán Thornton, a tough little guy, and son of Martin Thornton, a British heavyweight champion boxer also known as the 'Connemara Crusher' and one of Spiddal's extraordinary characters of the era. My other friends were Joe Francis, whose family ran Francis' grocers, where my mother shopped, and Éamon Hughes, whose family ran Hughes' Bar, where my dad liked to drink.

'I have my own protection squad,' I used to boast.

I felt very comfortable in life. Like most children, I wasn't fond of school, but school was just a small part of the day and the rest of the time I was free. My parents were loving people, and they couldn't have been stronger or more affectionate. One of the strange things about life is that the whole is often greater than the sum of the parts, and that principle certainly applied with my family.

In those early years a lot of activities began in our yard. My friends called to me because my parents were easy going and we had plenty of toys. The summer I was seven, I was allowed to travel for miles with a friend along the roads of Connemara on a rusty bicycle with no tyres. (Even today, when I catch 'Last of the Summer Wine' on television, I can't help crying, 'There's my bike!') Another time, my father lifted me up onto his donkey, dropped a wrapped sandwich into one of the big turf baskets, known as 'creels', hanging either side of the saddle, and let me off exploring on my own for the day.

At home, I felt I was allowed into an adult world. This was principally because I was at the tail end of a big family, but it also helped that by the time I was eight, the main topic of conversation was the construction of our new house. My parents had decided it was time to replace our

Thirteen Acres of Rock

three-roomed stone cottage with a bungalow with modern toilet and bathroom facilities – 'bringing all our outsides inside', as they used to say. I remember the day the architect called in and sat down at the table with my parents to explain everything – although looking back, I have a feeling the 'architect' may have been a glorified salesman, selling off-the-shelf plans from a catalogue.

The building work started in the spring of 1963. We had a local builder, Pat Mhicheálín, but the agreement was that my father, who was in his mid-fifties, would do most of the labouring. The biggest challenge was the preparation of the site. There were three huge rocks sticking out of the ground where my parents wanted to put the house, and they were too close to the old cottage, where we were still living, to be blown up with dynamite. Every morning for weeks on end, my father lit fires on the rocks. The heat would soften the rocks slightly so that by the evening he and another three or four local men with sledgehammers could have a go at them.

Through that build, I got to understand the character of my father. He really wanted to build that house, but when it came to each decision, he was afraid to put his toe in the water. He had to think about everything for weeks on end. My mother was the opposite; she just went for what she wanted, and worried about the details later.

Pretty soon, Pat Mhicheálín got to know my father's ways and he started

A late 1950s snapshot of a young Martin and Barbara shielding their eyes from the sun on their family land in Spiddal.

Never Know Your Place

to come to me.

'Sure, I'll talk to you, Martin,' he'd say. 'At least you'll give me an answer!'

In the end, there was not a block in that house that I wasn't involved in. I put hours of thought into the views from the windows and the positioning of the bedroom doors. My father began to defer to me on such matters. I had always been quick to give orders to other children, but this was the first time I'd ever given orders to my elders and I enjoyed it.

The house was finished on schedule in the summer of 1963, and for two months, as the date of our inevitable departure for Baldoyle grew nearer, I wallowed in the grown-up luxury of our new home. The shower and the toilet, the big new bedroom I shared with my brother Pádraic and even the grandeur of having a parlour (though I soon learned that, basically, a parlour was a lovely room you never got to use).

Mine was a contented life and I dreaded being sent away from it. I knew it was on the advice of the young female doctor who had taken over the practice in Spiddal and for whom Maureen was working as a secretary.

'She's a very progressive doctor,' my mother said. 'Look how she's kept working since she got married.'

My mother started to use new terms, which she said in English, like 'educational benefit', 'intensive physiotherapy', 'medical support' and 'safety'.

A couple of months before, Barbara had fallen in the classroom and I began to understand that we were considered too delicate for the rough and tumble of the local national school.

I didn't question my parents because they believed they were doing the best for us, and I could see they were filled with sadness at letting us go. But, yes, in later years I often thought, more with curiosity than regret, how different my life would have been if I'd stayed in Spiddal.

Chapter 3

Other People's Rules

In the hospital bedtime came early, long before dark fell, and the nights were long. I lay awake for hours, tuning into the sounds outside, trying to build pictures of the world beyond the hospital walls. Dogs barked all night on the little streets and occasional drunken voices could be heard as men returned home to their terraced cottages. Whose dog is that? I wondered. Whose voice?

It had only taken a day or two for Barbara and me to understand that our new life was to be governed by strict routine. Each morning, we rose at 7am along with the 130 or so other children. I had been given a wheelchair by the doctor, having presumably been deemed a hopeless case as far as walking was concerned, and it was parked beside my bed. We dressed as quickly as we could and one of the deaf boys pushed my wheelchair as we traipsed across the square to the cramped and warm chapel building where we huddled for 7.30am Mass.

Barbara and I slept in separate dormitories – it was strictly girls upstairs, boys downstairs – and the first thing I did each morning was look around the chapel to see if she was there. A night seemed so long.

'She's made it,' I'd say to myself when I spotted her.

Afterwards, we came back to the main building to have our breakfast,

Never Know Your Place

which consisted of watery porridge or very hard-boiled eggs. Our bread came buttered, and that meant butter underneath as well as on top – it must have sat in soggy stacks in the kitchen for hours before it was served. Only the tea was pleasant, but it proved someone in the kitchen knew how to do something right.

Immediately after breakfast, Nurse Murphy, the head day nurse, supervised as we queued for various inspections. Her deputy, Nurse Glynn, was chief nit-checker. When I reached her, she'd grab my chin and hold it firmly with her left hand while she drove the coarse brush through my hair, digging the needles into my scalp. She then applied mercurial wound ointment to any scabs or sores.

There was a second queue to have our boots inspected by the local cobbler, Al Neehan. The majority of hospital children used 'callipers' – rigid metal and timber braces which ran from their boots to their hips and enabled them to walk with crutches. The wear and tear and constant falling caused by these uncomfortable devices meant lots of boot repairs were needed, but the expense was never questioned because these walking children were seen as proof of the hospital's success.

Al Neehan examined each boot, buffing them as he did it, and took the damaged ones away with him to his tiny shop on the Baldoyle Road, where they said he and his assistant Kevin Shields worked by candlelight in a dark backroom to repair them. They were returned the same evening. It was all super-efficient, almost militaristic. Most children had two pairs of boots, but those who didn't were put in a wheelchair for the day.

All this happened before 8.15am, when we trundled the twenty yards to the hospital school, and we were handed over to our kindly lay teacher, Mrs Clarke, whose job it was to get Barbara and me speaking English.

Other People's Rules

Kit ducked in and out of the classroom all day, collecting children for physiotherapy sessions and dropping them back afterwards. This distraction was tolerated because there was an understanding that physiotherapy took priority over education, which was considered of limited use to children like us who had few prospects in life.

The hospital had been set up for children with polio (Little Willie, who Barbara and I discovered was now a teenager, was one of these). Though polio had been more or less eradicated, the polio treatment ethos remained. It was all about keeping children warm, feeding us, giving us plenty of physiotherapy, and of course looking after our souls so we would be ready when our time on earth (likely short) came to an end.

My first physiotherapy session was a scary experience, but I soon got to grips with this daily procedure. Kit came for me at 9am in his green porter's coat and favourite Aran hat. He wheeled me to the modern physiotherapy room, where I clambered out of my wheelchair onto a bench. The physiotherapist rolled me onto my face and then a leather strap was put around me and sandbags placed over my ankles to keep them straight.

To help pass the time until my release at 9.50am, Kit set up a chess board on a table near my head.

I soon learned that Kit lived with his wife, his mother (who worked in the hospital kitchens) and five daughters in a small cottage beside the rather grand parish priest's house and about ten yards from the hospital gates.

'I am blessed among women, Martin,' Kit said, straightening his Aran hat.

'But if there's an argument between my girls, I send them into the back garden and stay out of it,' he added, smiling down at me.

Never Know Your Place

'I have five sisters,' I told him.

'You'll know how it is, then,' he said.

While we played, Kit told me about the latest goings on in Baldoyle village: who'd won on the horses at the Baldoyle Races; who'd been out lamping for crabs on Dollymount Strand the night before and how many they'd caught; who hadn't settled a bill they'd run up at the pub. I didn't know the people he spoke about, but I liked to imagine their faces and be reminded of the dramas of ordinary life.

I kept an eye on the clock on the wall and became known for my distinctive west of Ireland plea to the physiotherapist.

'Miss, it's tin to tin, leh me go!'

Lunch break was 12–1pm. You'd know the day of the week by the smell emanating from the kitchens. Mince dinners of every sort were the speciality, served with mash. (At the beginning, the mash was real, but at some point later on it was replaced by horrible, powdered Smash.) Friday was always fish – a bland baked fish that tasted nothing like the fresh fish I'd been used to at home in Spiddal. I longed for the home-grown food I'd enjoyed in Spiddal, and above all for the taste of bacon, which for some reason never made it onto the Baldoyle menu.

School hours ended at 3pm, and it was only then that I felt good things could happen. The highlight was being called by the head nurse to 'Line up for your hash!'

'Hash' in those days referred to the small edible goodies that had been received from Saturday visitors over the previous weeks, which had been collected and stored away on our behalf and were now returned in daily rations. If a child was lucky, they might have a whole bar of chocolate to collect. If they weren't so lucky, they might get half a biscuit.

Other People's Rules

Barbara and I did better than average because our parents saw to it that we received a steady stream of visitors. Any Spiddal person who came to Dublin was duty bound to call to us at least once. We might not know who they were, but they would introduce themselves and explain how we were connected.

Our supply of Saturday visitors was to be aided in the years that followed by Galway's GAA success. In 1963, they made the football final and from 1964–1966, they were the All-Ireland Football Champions three years in a row. Many a time, I mentally thanked the team for their effort because it led to the provision of regular chartered trains, known as 'the excursions', which got everyone to Dublin cheaply for the matches.

Micheál Ó Bríain was our most regular visitor. A week after dropping us to Baldoyle, he came back to see us, and he returned every second Saturday. He came on his bike, often straight from a rehearsal at the Abbey, and in his canvas rucksack he brought two packets of Tayto and some comics. I had no interest in reading comics, but I didn't tell Micheál this because they proved invaluable for trading in the yard, which was one of my favourite pastimes.

Micheál was a brilliant storyteller and Barbara and I sat contentedly beside him, listening and eating our Tayto, so we wouldn't have to hand them in. He could convince us that Galway's football brilliance was all down to a few extraordinary players from Spiddal, who were single-handedly winning games. It filled us with pride to think it was Spiddal men who were bathing Galway in glory, although part of us knew it couldn't all be true. Micheál would then move on to a day-by-day account of what had happened in Spiddal that week – information he seemed to know in great detail despite the fact he lived in Dublin.

Never Know Your Place

Spiddal native Micheál Ó Bríain (right) in Brian Friel's *The Enemy Within*, staged by the Abbey Theatre, Dublin, in 1962, also starring Ray McAnally and Pat Laffan.

In the tough first years at Baldoyle, Micheál was our main connection to the outside world. I still remember his telephone number. He lived relatively close by in Beaumont and though he didn't have a car, he cycled over if we needed anything.

Phone calls from our sisters were another link to life outside the hospital walls. I laugh when people talk about conference calls as if they are a wonderful modern invention, because in my family they were a regular event in the 1960s. Maureen left her job with the doctor to become postmistress of Spiddal, and she would connect with Mairéad, who had started working in the GPO in Galway, and with Cait, who soon after got a job in the GPO

Other People's Rules

in Dublin, and they'd ring Barbara and me. Occasionally they'd even connect with Chris in America, but that was serious shit – they could have got sacked for that. Barbara and I held the receiver between us and didn't say much, but listening to our sisters talk made us feel part of the family.

Without those lifelines, the early years in Baldoyle would have been unbearable. It was misery to live every aspect of our lives under one roof, surrounded by the same people from dawn to dusk. In Spiddal, when I'd had a bad day at school, I could come home and be completely at ease. Now when something went wrong at school, that sense of failure covered everything.

I envied ordinary children. On fine afternoons, we were lined up in regimental rows of wheelchairs on the hospital forecourt to get the air, and from there we watched the village children being let out of the local national school at half past three. After a quick genuflection in front of the Church, they sprinted across the road to the hospital railings and stared back at us for a few minutes before going on with their day.

To them, our physical conditions must have seemed mysterious. If they asked, parents or teachers probably mumbled something about 'the handicapped', the 'great work of the nuns' or 'there but for the grace of God'. We lived alongside each other in the same north Dublin village, but our lives were entirely segregated, and they knew as well as we did that it is not for children to question the way things are.

The head nun, Sister Margaret Bernadette, or 'the White Tornado' as she was nicknamed, was the highest authority in the hospital and had an all-seeing eye. Dressed in white from head to toe, the White Tornado's swift and decisive hand governed all aspects of the hospital, instilling fear into children and staff alike. On a bad day, she could have given Nurse

Never Know Your Place

Ratched from *One Flew Over the Cuckoo's Nest* a run for her money.

Even the toilets displayed notices saying, 'These toilets are by order of SMB', as if to assure us that she had authority over even our most private functions. At mealtimes, she flew around, making sure we ate, and when she required attention, she whistled, leaving no doubt as to who was in charge.

On rare occasions the White Tornado would change her white shoes to black ones, which signalled she might be going into town for a few hours. That was cause for celebration, although the head ward nurse, Nurse Jones, was a fierce deputy.

Nurse Jones and her second-in-command Nurse Wade were the most hands-on in our care. Being a ward nurse was a residential job and both Jones and Wade were unmarried and had dedicated their lives to their work, living in the hospital since the 1940s when it had been just a few army huts. In Nurse Jones's case, we got the bitter end of this, but Nurse Wade was a kinder person, old-fashioned and almost regal in her persona, who would tell us about the offers of marriage she'd turned down in her youth.[3] Her softness encouraged us to play jokes on her, whereas with Nurse Jones it was just, 'Yes, Nurse. No, Nurse.'

The ward nurses were supported by day and night nurses who worked shifts but didn't live in the hospital. One night nurse walked around with a red plastic bat to reprimand children who didn't react quickly enough when she shouted, 'Get into line.' One night she caught a boy sneaking back from the hospital kitchen with a bottle of milk up his jumper and gave him such a wallop that the bottle fell to his feet and smashed.

Trouble-makers – and the awful thing was that often meant children who had intellectual as well as physical disabilities – risked being locked

Other People's Rules

in the 'Rumpus Room', a designated room on the first floor for those who couldn't 'control their behaviour'. I'd heard all about it from the boy who took the milk. It had padded walls and shuttered windows, and if a child was really wild and considered a danger to staff, they might be in there for hours – staff peering in at them through a little internal window – and at meal times, the hospital orderly would open the door so a nurse could slide in a tray.

The orderly was the staff member who did most of the physical jobs – like lifting older children on and off the toilet or in and out of baths. There were no hoists in those days so it was physically demanding work, and the orderly could be very gruff. I was sensible enough to anticipate his moods and stay out of his way, limiting my fluid intake to reduce the toilet visits, making sure no sloppy food was spilt on my clothes. But come 4.30pm, there was no escaping him as he rounded up the younger children and put us to bed before his shift ended. It was a rushed and perfunctory process, with none of the physical gentleness or soft words I had experienced at home and concluded only by the familiar sound of his Blue Austin Cambridge pulling out of the car park at five past five.

But amongst all these staff, it was an elderly nun called Sister Assissian who was the most sinister presence in my life. Two or three afternoons a week, Sister Assissian arrived at the door of the common room, where the boys gathered to watch television when there was a free hour, and beckoned us out with her wrinkled forefinger for some 'religious education' in one of the empty classrooms. In the thirty minutes that followed, her sole objective seemed to be to scare us stiff by twisting the gospel and enriching it with terrifying stories of evil communists. I'd never heard of McCarthyism, but she filled our minds with the idea that communists were everywhere:

Never Know Your Place

peering in through the classroom windows when our heads were down; watching us through the railings when we were in the yard. Perhaps her intention was to dampen our curiosity about the world outside. She certainly had a vivid and perverse imagination, and her stories haunted my nights.

It was not long before Sister Assissian died. She was the first dead person I ever saw, and looking into the open casket at her funeral, I lowered my head and prayed to God to ask some questions of her when she got to wherever she was going.

Chapter 4

The Batmobile

On Monday, 3 August 1964, the day finally came for Barbara and me to go home to Spiddal for our first holiday. I remember Jim Reeves's crashed plane had just been found, and when I was taken back to the ward after breakfast, the day nurses were passing a newspaper between them.

Ten months had passed without seeing my mother and father – visits from parents in a child's first year being strongly discouraged by the White Tornado, who deemed them unsettling.

It was my sister Chris, home from America for a holiday, who travelled on the train to collect us that morning. She was waiting in the family room at the end of the corridor and Barbara was already sitting beside her.

I watched Chris's expression change as the day nurse wheeled me in. She leaned over and hugged me into the stiff wool of her blazer, and looking half at the nurse behind me, she asked, 'Were you not sent here to get stronger and learn to walk better?'

Chris held my wrists and instructed me to stand up, telling the nurse crossly that we didn't need the wheelchair and the three of us struggled all the way home to Spiddal without it.

When we arrived in Spiddal that evening, the news that I had stopped walking was upsetting to my parents. They saw it as evidence of a decline in

Never Know Your Place

my health and began to question whether they had been right to send us to the hospital in the first place.

'I don't understand it,' my mother said, as she sat at the table and began peeling potatoes for the bacon dinner she had promised me.

My dad sat beside her, silent, and eying me softly as he chopped his home-grown turnip and cabbage.

'Don't the adverts always say the Little Willie Hospital gives lame children a chance to walk?' my mother continued.

I sat indoors for a week while the matter was debated. My mother's English was limited, and with my father preferring to avoid confrontation, they must have decided against contacting the hospital to ask questions. But as they observed my efforts to get around the house, which being a bungalow was not very challenging, they realised that walking wasn't an option, and somehow a wheelchair was procured so I could enjoy the rest of the summer.

Being in a wheelchair didn't affect my confidence. Quite the opposite. I was relieved at no longer being expected to struggle around the rocky ground on my unsteady feet. And after surviving the hospital regime, I was fearless. My wheelchair was my Batmobile.

Seán Thornton and Éamon Hughes propelled me at speed around the village. With a cigarette on my ear, I took dares and bets. We sneaked into the uninhabited cottages that lay everywhere like eerie theatre sets, abandoned when the owners took the boat to America with no more than a suitcase. A teapot might still be on the table or the sheets on the bed.

One evening, we held a barbecue in the graveyard, until some teachers from the village school got wind of it and came along to interrupt the fun. Everybody scarpered except me – partly because I couldn't, but also because

The Batmobile

I was not afraid of a few teachers who could do nothing except report me to my parents.

My father was cross when he heard, but after talking it over with my mother for a few minutes, he concluded – as he always did – 'In the interests of peace, Nora, let it be.'

Summers in Spiddal were wonderful. The village came alive as everybody arrived to learn Irish. First we had the Holy Joes – the priest and nuns – and then the crowd got younger and brighter as school children came. The final group was the older people, and by older I mean Leaving Certificate students and teachers. My parents took in lodgers – sometimes as many as ten – and every week there were new people to meet and learn about. Some came from wealthy farms, and I listened at the kitchen table as they talked

Spiddal Irish College in a 1950s/60s postcard. This postcard is from the collection of local historian Michael J Hurley who volunteered in Baldoyle Hospital in the late 1960s and recalls camping in Martin's father's field in Spiddal to attend Irish college.

Never Know Your Place

about their modern farming techniques in the hope they might be able to offer some tips for my father and his paltry acreage.

There was so much going on in Spiddal, and as the new postmistress Maureen was at the centre of it all. The post office was at the top of a hill on the edge of the village. We joked it was like Rome, with all the nuns rushing in and out.

The postmaster Mike Connolly, or Mikey as we all called him, was a real character, fierce nosey and with an opinion on everything. In those days the postmaster and postmistress could listen in on telephone calls, and Mikey was known for doing that. And it wasn't just listening, sometimes he would interject! Mikey had a piece of advice on every subject. If someone was hesitating or procrastinating, his voice would come on the line:

'Now if that was me, I wouldn't wait for the tide to come in. I'd busy myself going out to meet it!'

When summer drew to a close and it was time to return to Baldoyle, my parents hated it as much as we did. My mother tried not to show her tears and busied herself flicking over the calendar and making arrangements to visit us, and my father made hay in the big field because he couldn't bear to watch us go.

Chapter 5

Bottom of the Heap

In Baldoyle Hospital there was an unspoken understanding of who among the children had *nobody*, who had people *hardly worth talking about*, and who had people who might be *somebody*.

Kathleen Egan was one of those who had nobody. She was only a little younger than me but had been in the hospital since she was just four days old. She didn't know her parents and had to make do with visits from the charitable strangers the hospital encouraged to visit by placing adverts with children's photos in the newspaper. Kathleen had become the favourite of one such person, a mild-mannered Lufthansa pilot, who called by when he had a night stop-over in Dublin Airport.

'Here's my pilot!' Kathleen called, loud enough for us all to hear, whenever he turned up.

Kathleen took a two-year-old boy who also didn't have family under her wing. He sat on her lap for much of the afternoon. I suppose it softened life on both sides.

A few years after my arrival at Baldoyle, a little boy called Hubert McCormack joined us from rural Longford. He was only about three years old. I learnt later that his story was similar to my own – his mother had brought him to the doctor because he wasn't doing all the things his twin

Never Know Your Place

brother was, running around and all that, and the advice had been to send him to Baldoyle straightaway. Hubert and his mother were very close, and the first year or two, when few visits were allowed, broke his heart. All he seemed to say was, 'I go home please, Sister?'

Hubert later became friends with a girl called Rosaleen McDonagh, who was from a Traveller family in County Sligo, and arrived at the hospital when she was around four. Rosaleen was also from a loving family with a rich, rural way of life. Many of us felt that huge cultural divide between our rural homes and the hospital, but without question, the staff showed Rosaleen less respect than they showed the rest of us.

Though our vulnerabilities were there for all to see, there wasn't much teasing amongst the children. If a child was lucky enough to have parents with social standing, staff might be quicker to listen to the mother's concerns or allow an extra visit, but ninety-five percent of the time that child was in the same boat as the rest of us. The one thing we all had in common was our disability, and because of that we were all at the bottom of the heap in society, no matter what our father's name was.

My parents visited twice a year, usually on our birthdays. They brought me and Barbara clothes they'd worked hard to afford, but after they left, the clothes were often taken away to be shared with the other children.

This happened to everyone. In some ways, you could say it was fair because there were children like Kathleen with no one to bring them anything. But in other ways it was very cruel because those small reminders of our connection with our parents and our outside identity were taken away from us.

Low self-esteem pervaded and we talked about ourselves in a joking, derisory way. We called ourselves 'Muscies' (muscular dystrophy), 'Spiffs'

Bottom of the Heap

(Spina Bifida), 'Spas' (cerebral palsy), 'Quads' (quadriplegic) or 'Walkers' (deaf) – as if that was all there was to identify and divide us.

We knew we were there because society hadn't deemed us fit to grow up alongside our siblings and peers. To unburden our families – economically, physically, socially – we had been bundled off to the sidelines of life, where we couldn't be seen. No one expected anything of us. We were a bunch of little cripples in need of charity.

Except there were two people in the hospital who didn't buy into that.

The first was Kit Byrne, who had turned out to be so much more than a humble hospital porter. I'd never known a 'Kit' before, and it was an unusual name for an unusual man. Though he had little education, he seemed to see

Fundraising was an enormous part of life for staff and children in the hospital. Here nurses are pictured counting fundraising coupons collected and posted in from Lever Brothers laundry soap boxes. The supervisor is Nurse Wade, and in the background is Edward Power, Chairman of Baldoyle Hospital's Building Fund Committee.

Never Know Your Place

Kit Byrne, the hospital porter who looked out for the children and did what he could to raise their expectations.

ability in every child, encouraging us in his quiet way as he ferried us to and from physiotherapy.

There had been a pep in his step since Glasgow Celtic won the Scottish Cup final over Dunfermline in April 1965. He wanted to convince us we all had things to look forward to.

'I'm fattening the piglets for the holidays,' he told me as he pushed me to physiotherapy one morning in November 1965.

Soon all the hospital children knew that Kit was keeping pigs in a pen at the end of the long thin back garden of his cottage, feeding them on the slops from the hospital kitchen.

'One's to pay the meal-man, one for the coal,' he said, 'but the runt of the litter – well, that's going to be *my* money, to do what I like with.'

Bottom of the Heap

Kit made it clear he saw the runt as more of a challenge, but with a bigger reward. As the weeks passed, he delighted in telling us how the runt was coming along.

'Turns out she's as good as any of them, Martin!'

The drama in Kit's back garden escalated one Sunday in mid-December. Kit was working a half-day shift in the hospital laundry – something he often did to make a bit of extra money on his day off – when one of his daughters, Teresa, who must have been around nine, ran into the hospital.

'Where's my dad? Where's my dad?' she called in a panicked voice as she ran through the hospital towards the laundry. 'The runt of the litter's after escaping the pen. He's running wild in the garden. He has all of us terrified!'

Kit dashed off with Teresa, but was back less than ten minutes later, sweat on his brow.

'All under control, kids,' he said, nodding in the direction of various curious faces as he walked back towards the laundry. 'All under control.'

Kit must have decided we deserved a look at the spirited runt because the next afternoon when we were in the yard, he paraded her slowly past the hospital railings, using a bread board to steer her.

Somehow, the fact that this pig was going to be collected by the butcher's van the week before Christmas didn't detract from the cheeriness of Kit's homemade morality tale. We believed that it was the runt who saved his Christmas, and when we admired Kit's new Celtic jersey, we knew who deserved the credit.

The second person who softened the edges of life in the hospital was a volunteer called Dermot Mooney. He came in to visit the hospital children every Sunday, flushed and cheery in his neatly pressed white shirt and tie,

Never Know Your Place

carrying a box of Jacobs biscuits. He never missed it despite the fact he had a serious job as a manager in Odlums Flour Company on Alexander Quay and had four daughters of his own.

Kathleen Egan had gotten so fond of Dermot that she called him 'Mr Moo Moo' or 'My Da'.

Dermot's obsession with Glasgow Celtic was even greater than Kit's. Everyone knew he was a fanatical member of the Dublin branch of the Celtic

A Christmas party at Baldoyle Hospital on 16 December 1964, sponsored by Prescotts Cleaners and Dyers. Martin can be seen playing the tin whistle, Kathleen Egan stands directly behind him. Barbara is second from right in the back row and her best friend, Julie Cosgrove, is beside Martin.

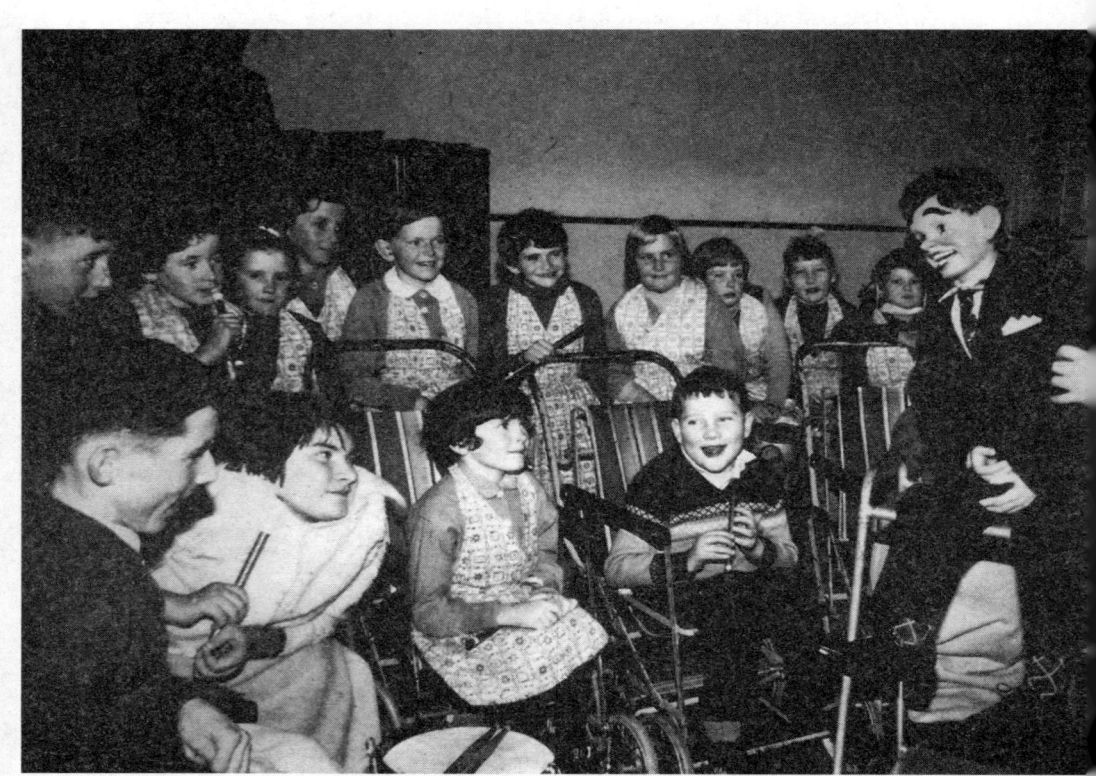

Bottom of the Heap

Supporters' Club, and on his tie he proudly wore a clover-shaped tie pin.

Dermot was also on the hospital fundraising committee, which meant he could pull strings with the White Tornado when he needed to. But it was more than that. He had a particular charm with the nuns. They appeared from backrooms when he arrived, and sometimes the White Tornado even signalled for an apple tart to be brought out with his tea.

'This is a fine apple tart, Sister,' Dermot would say and get stuck in with gusto.

Any goodwill he garnered was used for the benefit of the hospital children. It was Dermot who organised treats like the puppet shows and the annual Santa visit. When lads like me, aged eleven, looked embarrassed to join in, he pushed us good-humouredly.

'Go on up to Santa now, Martin. It won't do you any harm. You wouldn't want to insult him after he's come all this way.'

Dermot took the time to get to know all of us and that was extraordinarily rare in such a large institution. He wanted to know each child's story and he never forgot it.

When he saw me, he shook my hand, looked me in the eyes, and asked me a question that showed he remembered what was going on in my life. And while I talked, he wasn't afraid to rest his rugged hand on my shoulder, or to lift me out of my wheelchair and draw me in for a gentle hug.

Those hugs reminded me of the ones my parents gave me in the holidays, but there were some hospital children who wouldn't have known what a hug was if it wasn't for Dermot.

Chapter 6

Listening to the Lions

When you move to a new place, however resistant your heart and head may be at the beginning, there comes a point when you go from being an outsider to being an insider, and when the people around you – good and bad – become your people.

It's hard to say when exactly this happened, but by the time I was twelve or thirteen, I had some good friends amongst the children of the hospital. There was Georgie Nibbs, of small stature but with something of a resemblance to his namesake, footballer George Best. Georgie's family lived up the road in Donnycarney and he was a reliable wing man for any project I hatched. Another friend, John Doyle, had taken it upon himself to get my English vocabulary up to standard, using pirate radio as his main teaching resource.[4]

In Spiddal, I had been the leader of my gang and by 1967 I had reprised that role in the hospital. I spent my idle minutes devising ways to add colour to our days. I might as well live for the moment. After all, I didn't have much of a future to look forward to. My diagnosis was 'Duchenne' muscular dystrophy, and a boy with Duchenne's was destined for a short life. I'd seen other lads with the condition die after a cold or flu. The rest of us joked we were on death row. Every time one of us went, we all moved a

Listening to the Lions

step nearer to the front of the queue.

The imminence of death lent an urgency to everything, and that urgency was to have fun in spite of the White Tornado's authoritarian regime. The best way to do this was to devise a convincing excuse to invite outsiders into the hospital, or better still, to get ourselves beyond the hospital walls for a few hours.

The early years of the Hospital football team, c. 1967. Martin is in the centre. Martin's friend Georgie Nibbs stands to his left, wearing white. Dermot Mooney is top right. The other man is fundraiser Eugene Halton, and in the middle is Nurse Ellen O'Donnell.

Kit and Dermot had started a hospital football team made up of deaf lads or those with minor physical disabilities, and since I fancied myself as an expert on the rules, I'd been given the job of umpire. When Celtic became the first British team to win the European Cup in April 1967, our collective enthusiasm for the game reached new heights. Dermot Mooney,

Never Know Your Place

who lived to put a smile on our faces, must have seen this and somehow he used his contacts in the Celtic Supporters' Club to convince the entire European Cup team to visit the hospital.

It was St Patrick's Day, Sunday, 17 March 1968.

'God knows how he's done it,' Kit said to me that morning after Mass as he busied himself tidying up the yard.

Most of the staff were in, even those not scheduled to work, and it was all hands on deck to get the hospital looking its best.

Kit continued, 'I mean, you know yourself, lads in the village would walk over fire to meet the Lisbon Lions.'

'Do you really think the whole team will come?' I asked. 'When will they be here?'

The day before had been my fourteenth birthday and my mother and father had visited, so I was revved up already – and now this!

'Don't take it as gospel, Martin,' Kit said, 'but what I've heard is they will be going to meet de Valera in the Phoenix Park and might be squeezing us in beforehand. They've the game against Shamrock Rovers at Dalymount Park tomorrow, so it has to be today.'

Manager Jock Stein, Captain Billy McNeill and the Celtic team arrived in a coach an hour later, and the White Tornado herself rushed across the yard to the coach door to welcome them as they disembarked. After handshakes and a walk around the wards with the huge European Cup in arm, they gathered again in the hospital yard. Stein nodded to Billy McNeill and the team started to play football with us. It was electrifying. Like the huge spotlight that shone over those men had suddenly illuminated us in our hidden corner of Dublin.

McNeill stopped playing every now and again to offer tips.

Listening to the Lions

'Always pass the ball ahead of a player,' he said, 'so he can keep running, rather than to him.'

Jimmy Johnstone made us practise dropping the ball from the flat roof of the hospital building onto the concrete yard below, to learn how to control it.

'Kill the ball dead when you receive it!' he yelled.

I say 'us' because that is how I remember it. It felt like we were all involved, even though as a wheelchair user I couldn't play. But I memorised every word that day, every piece of advice, and not long after I became the unofficial manager of the hospital's football team. I was proud when the other kids nicknamed me Jock Stein after Celtic's brilliant manager and strategist. The man who took a bunch of players from disadvantaged backgrounds and 'bred' success into them. Yes, Stein was the kind of man I wanted to be. A man who focused on the strength and victory of his team, rather than individual success.

The Celtic visit was more than just a wonderful day in our otherwise bleak lives. We might have been at the bottom of the heap in society, but the fact that these extraordinary men, who had the respect of the whole of Europe, knew who we are – well, that gave us hope. We hadn't been forgotten. We were part of the world and things might happen.

The hospital football team became a chink of light in our lives. It turned out we had plenty of athletic young lads – like the Cruise brothers from

Irish President Éamon de Valera with Celtic Manager Jock Stein, Captan Billy McNeill and the European Cup. Taken at Áras an Uachtaráin on 17 March 1968, the same day the Celtic team visited Baldoyle Hospital.

Never Know Your Place

North Dublin (if you had those boys on your team, you weren't going to lose) or the affable Pat Crossan from Donegal (watch the windows!). Seeing them play better each week gave us something to root for, an outlet for the pent-up energy we had inside.

The Celtic team sent us proper socks, nicks and jerseys, and Kit and Dermot started arranging friendlies in the hospital yard against local teams. Two village boys, who I'd watched kicking a ball outside the railings, even asked permission to join the team.

'This is some turnaround,' I said to myself.

My job as team manager was to set targets, and if we won, to ensure every kid in the hospital shared the joy of victory.

'Our fans are everything,' I told people. 'Like they are for Celtic.'

On the surface, everything I did was about football, but really it was about livening up our lives and blurring the boundaries between the hospital and the world outside. I spent hours strategising. I volunteered for a fundraising walk because it gave me an opportunity to meet Joe 'Jawser' Ryan, the principal of nearby Portmarnock School. During the walk,

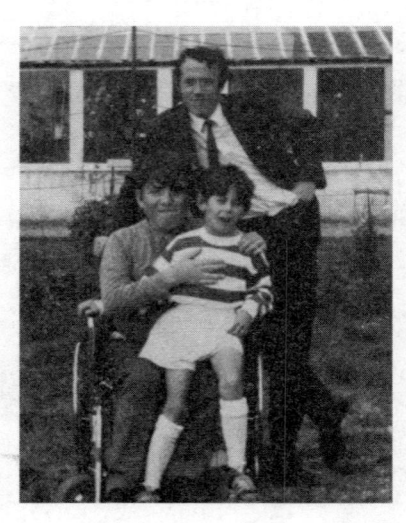

Martin with an unidentified young player on the hospital football team and a volunteer called Pat Norris. Several volunteers helped Kit and Dermot with the hospital football club in its first years (other regular volunteers at that time included Michael J Hurley, Billy O'Meara and Tom Farrell).

Listening to the Lions

I convinced Jawser that his school team should be playing ours on a regular basis. Jawser agreed and four home games and four away games were added to our calendar.

The only challenge was justifying to the White Tornado our quarterly bus excursions to the away games. Even if she had said yes before, I didn't know if she'd agree the next time. But Kit was a useful ally. He knew he was indispensable to the running of the hospital, and he had a quiet charm. He went at her from one angle and Dermot from another, and if we needed back-up, we'd arrange for Jawser Ryan to drop by unannounced.

While we had no choice but to seek permission for big things such as bus trips, when it came to minor transgressions or stretching of the rules, Kit, Dermot and I conspired to get away with what we could unseen. It was often easier to get forgiveness than permission. The secret to change, I concluded, was to push the limits and live to see another day.

It helped that I had made myself useful to the White Tornado by joining the fundraising committee and volunteering for collections. Once my English was as good as my Irish, I was only too happy to sit for hours outside Clery's on a Saturday, engaging with every passer-by. It was a joy to be free and have adult conversation and an occasional cigarette, not to mention real egg and chips at the Pillar Café on O'Connell Street.

I had become such a good collector that the Tornado sent me up and down the country on the train for important collections, and every Monday evening I was locked in a room in the hospital and entrusted with the task of counting the money that had been collected over the weekend.

I knew that if I was going to get the things I wanted, I needed the support of the Tornado, so I was careful to be spotted in the right places, to be quick organising the collection licences for the following weekend and to be the first to give her news about how much we had collected. It wasn't hard to impress her. She valued organisation, industry, action – and these were all principles I was prepared to take on. She started to see me as someone who could help her hit her fundraising targets, and on rare occasions she let her guard down. One Monday evening, after I'd informed her of the weekend's totals, she let slip that she had come to her vocation later in life and had worked in hotel management before joining the order.

As a young child I used to cry to get my father to give me what I wanted, and those manipulative instincts came alive in me again as I ingratiated myself with the White Tornado. It was an animal instinct, honed because my happiness depended upon it. Nonetheless, there was an honesty in our exchanges. The Tornado wanted something I could give her, and I wanted something in return.

The September after I turned fourteen, the Tornado gave me permission to attend the local girls' school, St Mary's Secondary School, so I could do my Leaving Certificate. I knew I was lucky. A secondary education outside the hospital, with a focus on serious learning rather than physiotherapy, was a privilege given only to children who had proven themselves worthy against the odds (or those whose parents shouted loudly enough).

Travelling the few hundred yards to the school freed me from the oppressive hospital routine. I was not an inmate anymore. I got to eat my meals at different times to the rest of the children. And the girls at the school, which included Kit's older daughters, gave me every piece of village gossip – much juicier than the snippets from Kit I'd survived on for years.

After school on Thursdays, I was asked to join Dermot, Kit and the hospital maintenance manager George Cosgrave on a committee to resurrect the defunct Baldoyle United Football Club. Our hospital football team was

Listening to the Lions

by now a fully-fledged member of the local league, playing against Bayside, Howth, Donaghmede, Sutton Park and Kilbarrack, but Kit said the players needed opportunities for progression.

'It will give them and the other lads round here something to get stuck into. Might even bring a bit of cheer back to the village,' he told everyone as he drummed up support. 'The lads'll be wearing green and white as a tribute to Celtic.'

This was the first time I'd been involved in a project outside the hospital walls, and it made me feel part of the village.

When my friend Georgie Nibbs, who was a good year older than me, turned sixteen, he moved back to his family home in Donnycarney. It was rare for a patient to return home, but Georgie's small stature didn't affect his mobility, and he'd managed to get a job in the hospital kitchens. I had never heard of a former patient being employed by the hospital, but I noted it was possible.

Georgie nipped in and out of the hospital each day on his Honda 50. His job proved handy because he slipped an extra slice of meat or bread into the bags on the back of our wheelchairs whenever he could (if that happened, you had to sneak off and eat it quickly).

Georgie and I had become the chief organisers of the hospital fundraising dances, which took place every few months. Sometimes we had a guest band – one time we even got the then little-known Thin Lizzy – but most often Georgie and his country band Elronde took centre stage. Georgie sat on a chair, his right arm hooked over his guitar, while the lead singer, a bushy-bearded lad from the village called Tom Farrell, belted out the tunes with Georgie on backing vocals.

One of my jobs was to invite the girls from my secondary school to

Never Know Your Place

the hospital dances. I was at an age when I was starting to feel alive to the world of women. As well as the girls at school, I was fascinated by the trainee nurses who cared for us in Baldoyle. Nicknamed 'bluecoats' or 'QAWs' (Qualified Arse Wipers) by the hospital children, most of them were only a year or two older than me and there was a natural curiosity.

With so many possibilities around me – football, friends, girls, not to mention cigarettes and the occasional smuggled beer – life started to feel very worth living. Lying in bed at night, I bargained with God.

'Just another year or two, so I can do something worthwhile with my life. Like help the hospital football team win the final.'

Then, in January 1969 when I was nearly fifteen, my turn on death row arrived. I came down with the Hong Kong Flu and it was accepted by everyone that this was it. The hospital doctor made it clear I was not expected to recover. There was no time for my parents to make it from Spiddal, but the priest came and I was anointed.

Just when everyone believed it was curtains, I surprised them by pulling through the next morning. They had been expecting a funeral and instead I was out of bed and looking for my breakfast. The doctor, who knew me well, threw his hands in the air and said to the nurse on duty, 'I don't understand. Just give him whatever he wants!'

That day, something in me told me that I was not going to die anytime soon. I didn't feel fragile. Until then, I had always been in a hurry, thinking about every project only in terms of the year ahead. Now it was different. I set myself a new goal: maybe, if things went really well, I could make it to thirty. It was an ambitious deal – a lot to ask of God – but I wanted to keep the show going as long as possible.

Chapter 7

Daring to Dream

'Win in a few games, but don't get carried away,' I told Kathleen Egan at our practice session in the hospital hall the day before her first wheelchair table tennis competition.

She narrowed her eyes and twiddled her bat but said nothing.

I kept going. 'I'll give you a signal when I want you to lose a game.'

I didn't want everyone finding out how good Kathleen was at her first event. It was all about the build-up. When she won every game at the same competition the next time around, everyone would get the impression it was down to the brilliant coaching I had given her.

Kathleen was one of the first serious athletes to emerge from the hospital sports club that Kit, Dermot and I had founded. Spurred on by the success of our hospital football team, we were trying to take things further.

Baldoyle Hospital Sports Club, or BHSC as we called it, marked a turning point in all our lives because through it we were loosening the White Tornado's grip. She had agreed that outside of school hours we could organise any sports activities we liked, including sports that suited children who used wheelchairs, like table tennis and shot put, providing we didn't demand any assistance from her staff. She was nothing if not pragmatic, and now in her sixties and starting to suffer ill health, she saw we had the

Never Know Your Place

Martin's friend Kathleen Egan (now Reynolds). Kathleen started playing table tennis in Baldoyle Hospital Sports Club and went on to compete in several Paralympic Games.

skills to take over a chunk of her work.

Away from her beady eyes, sport became the area in which we were freest to experiment. The hospital children gathered in the sports hall in the afternoons and at weekends, and this included girls like Kathleen, my sister Barbara and Rosaleen McDonagh, who until then had lived somewhat segregated lives in their ward on the first floor (it was a sore point with me that I'd never even seen where my own sister slept).

You could feel the energy in the air as young people who had been treated like invalids their whole lives discovered they had physical strength.

Kathleen, who was as fiery and free-spirited as they come, spent every free minute playing sport. If she wasn't in the hall, she was bouncing a ball at the bottom of a stairwell. Part of her joy was that she had finally been given a wheelchair, after being pressured by the staff to hobble around in callipers and crutches for much of her life.

'Why did they put me through that torture?' she asked me. 'It was such a waste of my time and energy.'

Barbara had also started using a wheelchair and watching her play table tennis with her best friend Julie Cosgrove, it was hard not to wonder about how misguided medical thinking can be. They pushed children to walk because it was the only measure of success that society understood, but many of us were freer when we used a wheelchair – even the badly designed ones the hospital gave us.

Kathleen was so agile that she could pick up serious speed by leaning forward and pushing the little wheels at the front of her wheelchair. If I needed to get somewhere fast, I grabbed onto the back of her wheelchair, and she pulled me along. Sometimes Barbara caught onto the back of mine, and the three of us moved in a train across the sports hall.

Never Know Your Place

Every day I coached Kathleen as she played table tennis against a boy called Michael Cunningham, or the 'blond dynamite' as we all called him due to his speed and golden good looks. Kit had hung the speakers of our record player on the hall wall and after practice, Kathleen, Michael and I lingered, pretending to tidy up while we blasted out Miami Showband records. We spent hours together in that sports hall, gearing ourselves up for the future. Kathleen started referring to Michael and me as her 'brothers'.

We knew the world outside the hospital was beginning to change. We'd seen reports of the Paralympic Games and the Stoke Mandeville Games in newspapers, and terms like 'inclusion' and 'integration' were appearing in the headlines. It was all ammunition to do more of what we were doing already.

Much as I liked a day out, bringing the hospital children to clubs and tournaments could be problematic. Too often we were singled out for special treatment, and while the non-disabled children were getting a clip around the ear, our lot sat in the corner of a sports hall drinking tea and eating custard creams. It was well meant but attracted attention to the ways in which we were different.

I concluded that integration worked best when we invited other young people to tournaments and social events at the hospital. It gave us the psychological advantage. The onus was on the visitors to adapt. Sometimes the effect proved magical. The visiting young people took time to observe and explore their curiosity about disability.

'What happened to your legs?'

'Why do you talk funny?'

'What's wrong with you?'

We didn't mind telling them anything they wanted to know. We were just happy they were interested in us.

We were lucky that every part of the hospital complex reached onto a public road. It was not hidden down a long avenue like many institutions. Housing estates were springing up around it and gangs of aimless children hung about on every corner. When we held matches, bored children had started wandering in to watch. On a good day, the hospital felt more like the heart of the village than the forbidding grey prison it once was.

My mission was to keep the doors open for as many hours of the day as possible, not just for the sake of the children in the hospital, but for the benefit of the whole village. If we started to think big and row in together – do things the Glasgow Celtic way – perhaps we could make more of all our lives?

To the White Tornado and broader authorities, I did everything I could to portray BHSC as an innocuous leisure initiative, but, in reality, it was a deliberately subversive entity. I hoped regular mixing with non-institutionalised young people would plant ideas in the minds of the hospital children. These ideas, I reasoned, would gradually erode the principles on which the hospital operated, namely fear and obedience, and the deliberate stifling of each child's sense of individual identity and connection to their family.

Kathleen had done what I asked and lost a few games in her first table tennis competition, and this slowly, slowly by-stealth approach paid off in 1969 when she astonished everyone by being selected, along with Michael Cunningham, for the Stoke Mandeville Games in England.

After the Games, Kathleen arrived back at the hospital, pale with exhaustion. Something had shifted in her while she was away. Before she went up from the sports hall to her ward, I watched her make up a sign to pin to the wall beside her bed. On it she wrote: 'DO NOT DISTURB OR

Never Know Your Place

I'VE GOT A SURPRISE FOR YOU!'

The surprise, she told me the following morning, was a hammer under her pillow.

'Good job they left me alone because if they'd tried to wake me at the usual time, I was going to wave it around and scare them.'

She was laughing hard.

'I don't care if they think I'm crazy, Martin. The Sisters of Cruelty are not telling me what to do anymore.'

You can't overestimate how the success of disabled athletes like Kathleen and Michael changed the way we saw ourselves as young disabled people. It was not just witnessing their physical prowess, it was seeing how sport changed a person's character and expectations, how it emboldened them.

And even if you weren't going to be a great athlete, you could get fit and strong. If you couldn't hold a table tennis racket in your hand, you could hold it in your mouth. If you were on crutches, you could stand in goals and deflect the football with one crutch. If you liked giving orders, you could learn to referee (Hubert McCormack, the young lad who had missed his mother so, was a wheelchair table tennis umpire by the time he was seven). You could focus on your abilities, as people say now. We may have been disabled, but we were as boisterous as any other bunch of children, and the opportunity to enjoy our physicality was a revelation. The gap between ourselves and other young people seemed to be lessening – and if we started to see ourselves differently, maybe we stood a chance of changing other people's perceptions?

I wanted to keep pushing the potential of sport, and I started to wonder if I could make a career for myself in the area. I knew that in another year or two I would be expected to leave the hospital and go to an institution for

Daring to Dream

disabled adults somewhere else in Dublin. I didn't want to go. In Baldoyle I had real 'turf', as my father liked to say, and an outlet for my emerging interests in sport, community, and what might now be considered 'disability activism' – though back then it was mainly about insisting the hoolies held by the new Baldoyle United FC were in wheelchair-accessible venues.

But career planning was unchartered territory for a disabled person in those days, so I kept my thoughts to myself. I didn't want people to think I was getting above my station.

Chapter 8

Head above Water

By 1971, the White Tornado was in her late sixties and visibly fading but struggling to let go. It occurred to me that maybe she didn't have anywhere to go.

Her final project, which she had fundraised for despite the scepticism of the hospital board, was the construction of a twenty-metre heated swimming pool. She was proud, even strangely joyous, the day it opened.

I volunteered to help her run it by working as a poolside attendant several mornings a week before school, and for a couple of sessions at the weekend. I had sharp eyes and an authoritative voice, and this was more important than being able to swim – which of course I couldn't. My time was valuable because the Tornado was under pressure to keep running costs down, and as the trainee nurses liked to swim in the morning after their night shift, it wasn't the worst job to wake up to.

One morning when I was not scheduled to work, I decided to head to the pool anyway. I kept glancing over at one of the trainee nurses who I had a soft spot for – she was from the North and had a lovely accent. After a while, I noticed she had gone down to the bottom of the pool.

'Jaysus, she's a great set of lungs,' I joked to a couple of nurses who were sitting on plastic chairs beside me.

Head above Water

Thirty seconds later, she still hadn't come up. I shouted across to one of the pool staff, Gussie Duggan, and he dived straight in and dragged her out. Kit must have been called because it was he who administered the kiss of life until she spluttered back to consciousness. She seemed fine and got herself up, but in the dressing room a few minutes later she went into what they call 'secondary drowning' and ended up being carted off to Jervis Street Hospital for two weeks.

The incident was considered a near miss. When the Tornado heard about it she called me into her office. She looked tired.

'I am very grateful you had your eyes on the pool and raised the alarm,' she said.

For a minute I thought she was going to lean over and give me a kiss, but she held back and opened the drawer of her desk, slipping me twenty cigarettes instead.

From that day on, as far as the Tornado was concerned, I was the boss of that pool. When my Leaving Cert results were not what I had hoped for – due largely to my extensive extra-curricular activities – she gave me special permission to stay on in the hospital for another year to repeat. I was told it would make me the oldest patient the hospital had ever had.

But by the time I was taking my Leaving the second time around, Barbara and several of my friends, including Kathleen and Michael, were in the process of moving to a newly built Cheshire Home in the Phoenix Park. It was looking like I would have to join them. I considered this most inconvenient for my social life. I had started hanging out with the off-duty trainee nurses and local teenagers on the Golf Links at Portmarnock Strand and had even commandeered my own spot at Grainger's Pub on the Main Street in Baldoyle.

Never Know Your Place

If the Tornado had still been there, she'd have found a way to keep me, but she had retired. Her successor, Sister Marie John, was a super-qualified but conservative character, who didn't have any particular loyalty to me.

While I wracked my brain for a way out, the hospital announced that due to inflation, it could no longer afford to heat the pool and would be closing its doors at the end of the year. The hospital children were disappointed, because pool sessions gave them a break from the monotony of the school day, as were many villagers, who used the pool in public hours.

I knew the pool could be run more efficiently if we got a team of local volunteers to help us, so I decided to draft a rescue plan and hand it to the hospital's buildings committee.

While they mulled it over, I took my chances and put it into action. It didn't take long. Local swimming instructors and parents came forward and agreed to give a few hours a week and to guarantee income by bringing in groups. We put together new programmes to cater for families in the housing estates, like children's classes, mother and baby classes, and ladies' night. I put a lot of energy into making my plan work, because I believed it would provide a secure footing on which to keep the pool open for good, doing justice to the work the Tornado put in. (Now she was gone, I admit I missed her a little.)

My rescue plan was also about proving I was more than just a resourceful kid. I understood money and could run the pool in a business-like fashion. Once the committee realised what I was capable of, I hoped they would see reason and give me a proper job.

But this process, like all processes that involve committees, took time, and I could no longer hold back the inevitable. I packed my records and clothes into my suitcase and Kit drove me in silence to the Cheshire

Head above Water

Home in the Phoenix Park.

The blow was softened by the fact that I was to be given a daily allowance of £5 by the hospital to fund the cost of a taxi from the Cheshire Home to the hospital every day.

'That will allow you to continue your voluntary work at the pool,' Sister Marie John said as she handed over the first fiver.

It was a small gesture, but I saw it as hugely symbolic: they were recognising they needed me and that my input had monetary value.

The Cheshire Home was located on a hill in the Phoenix Park, next to a hospital, and it came as a shock to find myself so far from the bustle of human life. It had only been open a few months and there was no denying

Martin is pictured, paperwork in hand, in front of the sign for Baldoyle Hospital Swimming Pool, which he saved from closure and played a key role in running.

Never Know Your Place

that it had modern facilities, but it was surrounded by parkland and cut off from the rest of the city. The steep hill and undulating lanes beyond were impossible to navigate in a wheelchair, and eerie after dark.

The hospital next door was for elderly people, and the building closest to our accommodation was the hospital morgue. We joked there was more activity in the morgue than in the hospital itself.

Late in the evenings, when we hung around the poorly lit grounds smoking, one of the lads, John Maguire, had a comic routine where he put his hands on the ledge of a high morgue window and pulled himself up out of his wheelchair to peer in.

'Come on now!' he started calling. 'Get up out of that! There's nothing really wrong with you!'

It was hardly a suitable place for people in their late teens and early twenties, all of us craving freedom and a social life. But the staff thought it was a marvellous facility. Leonard Cheshire himself arrived for an official visit and I told him straight, 'This place is a five-star hotel in the middle of the Sahara Desert!'

We each had dreams about how we would escape. My hopes revolved around getting Baldoyle Hospital to give me a proper job. Barbara talked about renting a flat one day with her friend Julie. Kathleen had her table tennis training and competitions, and she had also found a boyfriend from the outside.

My daily taxi to Baldoyle kept me going. 'Car 78' waited for me every morning, including weekends, because weekends were when the pool made most of its money. Freddie was my morning driver and John my nighter. I was their top customer, so on the way home on Saturdays John didn't object to a detour to Ballyfermot, where I picked up treats from our favourite

Head above Water

takeaway for Barbara and my pals. This ritual helped relieve the boredom of Saturday nights and let me hold on to some of my former influence. I can't remember what the takeaway was called, just that it was known to us as 'The Dog's Paradise', because as well as fish and chips and burgers, it sold the crubeens (pigs' feet) I had eaten as a child in Spiddal.

Chapter 9

From Patient to Taxpayer

In quiet moments I had a habit of making up rules to live by. I suppose it made me feel I was shaping my life, despite the limited options on the table.

My number one rule was to make the most of every opportunity, because you never knew when one thing might lead to another.

I had first put this rule into practice after the Celtic visit in 1968 when I had asked Dermot Mooney if I could join the Dublin Glasgow Celtic Supporters' Club. Dermot had duly arranged it and, sure enough, I'd ended up getting more chances to meet Billy McNeill and other players.

Billy McNeill had turned out to be a big man in every sense. Stature. Power. Personality. Heart. I noticed how he commanded any room he entered. He didn't need to raise his voice to be heard.

Billy took a shine to me, and on 3 March 1973, just before my nineteenth birthday, he arranged for me to fly to Celtic Park as his special guest to watch Celtic play Aberdeen.

I'd only been abroad once before – to Lourdes as a young child when my parents had taken me on the obligatory trip in search of a 'cure'. Flying to Glasgow with Dermot and a pleasant nurse called Ellen O'Donnell as my chaperone felt very exciting.

From Patient to Taxpayer

We arrived at Celtic Park a few hours before the match, and Billy greeted us and brought us into Jock Stein's office. It was clear he had told Jock about everything I was doing in the hospital and about my part in re-starting Baldoyle Football Club. Jock started talking about a concept he called 'success engineering'.

'People who grow up together have a sort of special power, Martin,' he said. 'You can achieve great things if you have a vision and get everyone to believe in it. It's all about community.'

The word 'community' stuck in my mind because those were the days before it was a buzzword. I liked the idea that power could come from the ground up.

Afterwards, Billy pushed me down the corridors of Celtic Park towards the locker room to meet the other players. He paused when we got to the door.

'Now you take it easy on these lads, Martin. Remember, you make them more nervous than they make you.'

Those few words from Billy changed how I thought about my disability. From that day on, when I entered any room outside the hospital, I reminded myself that the people around me were probably feeling more awkward than I was. My job was to put them at ease and then turn the situation to my advantage.

Not long after I came back from that trip Kit spotted an advert posted by the Department of Education in the newspaper: 'Candidates sought for an Irish delegation to a pioneering course in sports psychology and rehabilitation, to be held in Germany and the United Kingdom'.

One of Kit's many jobs was to drive Sister Marie John around, and when he had her ear, he showed her the advert and convinced her the course was

Never Know Your Place

Above: Martin on an Aer Lingus flight on his way to Celtic Park on 3 March 1973, beside Dermot Mooney and an unidentified member of cabin crew.

Below: Martin in front of the tunnel at Celtic Park with Celtic Captain Billy McNeill behind him and Dermot Mooney on the right, March 1973.

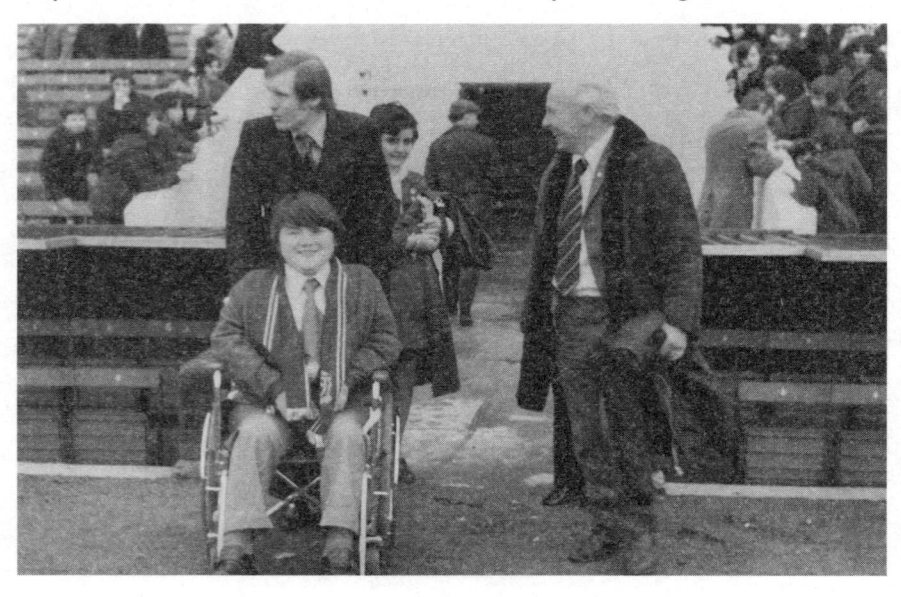

From Patient to Taxpayer

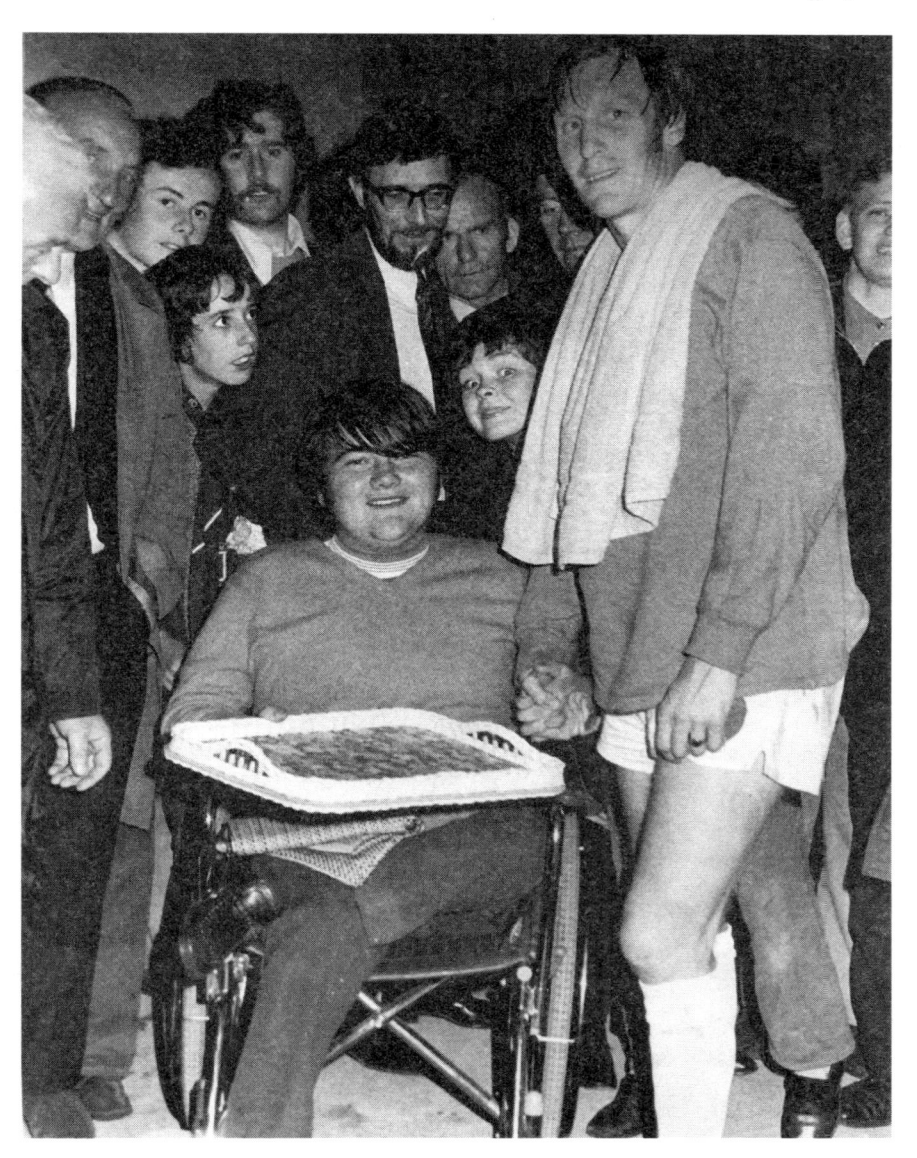

Martin with Captain Billy McNeill and onlookers at his visit to Celtic Park in March 1973. Celtic had just played Aberdeen.

Never Know Your Place

made for me. And Kit being Kit, he didn't just get her to write me a reference, he got her to submit the application on my behalf.

After several months, I got news I'd been selected. I was the youngest of the nine coaches in the delegation, and none of the others had a disability. It felt like a big break. Even when my wheelchair got lost by the airline on the way to Stuttgart, it didn't knock the enthusiasm out of me.

The first two months of the course were to take place at the Bad Wildbad Rehabilitation Hospital in the Black Forest, and we were housed in adjoining university accommodation. During the day, we attended a course run by Herr Professor Walter Weiss, an expert in wheelchair sport, and at night we hung out with the staff and students and drank lots of German beer and sweet white wine.

I had become a serious smoker and I kept a box of matches wedged down the side of my wheelchair, which I had to swing at with my arm, match in hand, trying to get as much height and velocity as I could, if I wanted to light up. This process was rather conspicuous, and I soon learnt that smoking indoors was a serious social offence in Germany. Rather than the offers of help I got in Dublin, I got an instant earbashing from students.

Beer on the other hand was acceptable any place, any time. Even at breakfast.

Walter Weiss was a tall, substantial man in his fifties, jolly but with limited English. He took us on road trips around Germany to see the impact sport was having on the well-being of disabled people. The main Irish delegation travelled in a bus behind Weiss' Saab, but as the bus wasn't wheelchair accessible, Weiss decided I had better travel in the passenger seat beside him.

Once he hit the autobahn, there was no stopping him. I gasped as he swerved to overtake yet another car.

'But we are in a hurry!' he said.

My stomach was on the floor, but I loved the feeling of speed on the open road.

At the programmes we visited, we saw people with spinal injuries doing every sport in manual and electric wheelchairs. Weiss kept drawing attention to how sport could influence the way disabled people felt about themselves.

'If they see themselves as a patient and not a person, they won't get anywhere,' he said.

Weiss often directed his points at me.

'Martin, I need people like you to spread the word.'

Weiss saw I was a person who needed a clear vision of what I was trying to achieve. I told him about my recent conversation with Jock Stein.

'He's absolutely right,' Weiss responded. 'You can "engineer" success. But first you must know what success looks like!'

As we sped along, we talked about being true to your vision and not hurrying, and the ways you could help others see it too.

'You can't describe change to people if they are afraid,' Weiss said. 'They just worry about what they might lose. Talking gets you nowhere. You need to show them.'

He continued, 'If someone is going around thinking, "I am disabled" or "I am excluded," you have to challenge them. Get them to discover new skills, go to places they thought they couldn't go. If you do that, they will find new words to describe themselves.'

Weiss nurtured ideas I had already been hatching. Yes, I thought: my instincts have set me on the right track. It reassured me that a free-thinker

Never Know Your Place

like Weiss was working in an institutional hospital not unlike Baldoyle Hospital – and like me, he was trying to change things from the inside.

After two months with Weiss, we flew to the UK for the final month at Stoke Mandeville Hospital, where the tutor was to be none other than the founder of the Paralympic Games, Jewish émigré neurosurgeon Ludwig Guttmann. I'd seen Guttmann on television and he was already a hero of mine.

We were scheduled to meet Guttmann on our second day, and the first afternoon was given over to settling into our accommodation. The hotel turned out to be completely wheelchair-inaccessible, so I made my way on to the hospital to ask whether they could give me a bed in the spinal injuries ward instead. The ward sister agreed, but rather than hang around all evening, I left my belongings beside my bed and headed out to hook up with some off-duty Irish nurses who had worked in Baldoyle years earlier.

I had a fantastic night partying with the nurses in their hall of residence, but my disappearance caused some distress to the ward sister who, having offered me the bed, had expected me to settle down for the night. The police were called, and a search party was sent out. When I returned to the ward (under my own steam) at about 1am, there was such a commotion that it seemed only fair to spice up the story of my antics for the benefit of the patients around me.

By the time I was introduced to Guttmann the following morning, news of my 'excursions' the night before had clearly reached him. Guttmann was a short, officious-looking man, whose sharp eyes inspected everyone around him through fine-rimmed glasses. He seemed rather amused as he looked me over, but said nothing and began talking to our group, while doing three or four other things at the same time. He referred periodically

From Patient to Taxpayer

Sir Ludwig Guttmann as pictured in the programme of the Toronto 1976 Paralympic Games, a few years after Martin had first met him.

to a neat-looking Irish lady who stood beside him taking notes. Every few minutes he wiped the sweat from his brow with a white handkerchief, and then shoved it back into his pocket, where it was left, half hanging out, until it was next required.

He took us on a tour of the big wards filled with spinal injury patients and showed us how the hospital was trying to make rehabilitation more bearable. He had retired a couple of years earlier but his commanding demeanour suggested he was still the boss of the place.

'Rehabilitation is hard, slow work,' he said. 'It's easy to see yourself as a failure because you see so little change on a daily basis.'

Guttmann had devised techniques to help patients measure their progress, including asking them to keep diaries where they were to record what they'd accomplished each day.

Guttmann said, 'Sport helps patients to start seeing themselves in a new way. If you can get that far, the rest will come over time.'

Guttmann knew the movement he had created was ground-breaking. He was challenging the idea that being in a wheelchair meant a short, unhealthy existence and encouraging people to manage their conditions and get back to ordinary life. There was an energy about him, the kind that comes when hope of life is discovered where there was none before.

The majority of the staff seemed to be Irish, and he introduced our delegation to a new Irish patient, a builder called Tom Cunningham, who explained he had been paralysed in an accident on a construction site.

'Our aim is to turn patients like Tom into taxpayers again,' Guttmann said.

Guttmann's eyes focused on me while he was talking to the group and he kept firing questions at me.

'And do you pay taxes, Mr Naughton?' he wanted to know.

That threw me at first, but his point was that paying taxes was the best measure of whether you were a contributing citizen, and it gave you rights you'd never get otherwise. He was in a cantankerous mood, but his argument hit home. I knew then more than ever that if I didn't get a proper job in the hospital, I'd be selling myself short – both in terms of my pocket and my standing in society.

After the tour of the wards, Guttmann took it upon himself to resolve my accommodation issue by telephoning the adjoining residential centre. This centre, which was a sort of half-way house for patients transitioning out of the hospital, was run by an Irish couple by the name of Brennan.

From Patient to Taxpayer

I listened as Guttmann gave my details to Mr Brennan. 'Martin Naughton, MD,' he began.

He was letting them know I had muscular dystrophy, but being more used to dealing with spinal injuries, this reference was lost on Mr Brennan, who assumed it stood for Medical Doctor. Guttmann realised the misunderstanding but said nothing, and for the next three weeks we shared the joke as I enjoyed special treatment from the Brennans, who marvelled at my success in life.

I arrived back in Dublin on a dreary early December day to find John Bruton, the then Parliamentary Secretary for the Department of Education, waiting at the airport to drive me to the National Rehabilitation Board in Ballsbridge for a debriefing session. He had heard the bus from the airport was wheelchair-inaccessible. I was touched by this human gesture.

When we arrived in Ballsbridge, I was handed an envelope addressed to 'Mr Martin Naughton'. Inside was a letter from the Board of Baldoyle Hospital, offering me a residential job as their first 'recreation manager'. It stated I would be responsible for organising all children outside of school and physiotherapy hours. At last. I heaved a sigh of relief as I placed the letter on my lap and read the words again.

Later that day, Kit came out to collect me, looking rather pleased with himself. We stopped off at the Cheshire Home to collect my things and drove straight to Baldoyle.

Yes, Baldoyle Hospital was the same old grey, familiar place, but it felt fresh because I was there by choice. Everyone was delighted to see me, and my leverage and power was now official. It was time to earn a pitman's pay for a pitman's job. I had pride and beer money. Taxes would be paid.

'I'd like to see your face now, Guttmann,' I thought.

Never Know Your Place

The next day as I sat in the staff room, struggling to fill in twenty pages of Revenue forms, I realised there was no escaping bureaucracy if I wanted to be a fully paid-up citizen.

Kit peered over my shoulders while he sipped a pint of milk, which he always drank for his ulcers, and he couldn't resist offering his twopence-worth.

'My advice to you is to claim for everything and they won't be long telling you what you can't have.'

Martin with trophies and certificates won by Baldoyle Hospital Sports Club members in sports such as football, swimming and table tennis. In his hand, he has a Cúchulainn Award, given to him by the Irish Wheelchair Association for his work in sport. A packet of Carrolls cigarettes is visible on Martin's lap. Photo likely taken in the early to mid-1970s.

Chapter 10

Something about Mary

Mary Llewellyn was one of the trainee nurses, the Qualified Arse Wipers, though when she heard the term she gave out yards to me for calling them that.

It was 1974. She was seventeen, I was twenty. The first time I saw her was in the pool on a Sunday afternoon in August. Her proud parents had dropped her at the hospital that morning. It was only up the road from her family home in Donnycarney, but she was revelling in her freedom.

'It's exciting to have a swimming pool,' she said as she held on to the pool-side ladder. 'I unpacked my few bits and pieces and grabbed my togs and headed straight here.'

She would have kept chatting, but I was there to teach a lesson.

'I'll see you at tea later,' I said.

I could see from her blank face that she didn't know the routine yet, but she worked it out and walked into the hospital dining room at 6pm.

I noticed straightaway how she lit up the room. She was right over to my table and there were no awkward silences.

'You'd talk to a lamppost,' I said to her.

'You're the same, yourself,' she said. She was right.

She told me straight: she'd never seen disabled people before. 'I'm quite

Never Know Your Place

Martin and his first girlfriend and lifelong close friend Mary Llewellyn on a night out in 1974.

nervous. Hope I'll know what to do and all that.'

But I could see from the start she was looking to broaden her outlook. 'There's room in the world for everybody,' she said.

In the week that followed, poor Mary had a baptism of fire. Like all the trainees, she was given the worst jobs by the older nurses, including helping wash and bath teenagers not much younger than she was.

We laughed about it a few weeks later.

'It was all a bit shocking,' she said. 'You know I'd never seen male anatomy before.'

Mary was from a big family, with one brother and a clatter of sisters, just like me. It turned out she was a decent speaker of Connemara Irish because her dad had sent her to the Gaeltacht three times.

Something about Mary

'Coláiste Lurgan between Spiddal and Indreabhnán,' she told me. 'I loved it there.'

She even listened to the same sort of music as me and supported Celtic.

Mary became friends with Kit Byrne's daughter Teresa, who had started as a trainee nurse at the same time. Teresa was full of sass because of who her father was, and when she got a half-hour break, she tore her uniform off and put on her jeans so she could meet her boyfriend, Bobby Ranson, in the local for twenty minutes.

'The other girls are calling her "the queen of the blue coats",' Mary told me, laughing.

There may have been a bit of matchmaking going on because Teresa started inviting Mary and myself out with her and Bobby. The four of us went to dinner dances and shows at the Old Sheeling Hotel in Raheny, where we saw performers like Red Hurley, Dickie Rock, or Twink.

Martin and Kit Byrne's daughter Teresa in Baldoyle Village in the mid-seventies.

Never Know Your Place

The trainee nurses, who were housed on the second floor of the hospital, were limited to two 'passes' a month if they wanted to stay out past half eleven, but Mary wangled extra nights by going home to stay with her parents.

Our favourite place if we went out on our own was the Camelot Hotel on the Malahide Road. If we ordered a taxi, Mary was able to push my wheelchair close to the back passenger door and then climb in on the other side and pull me out of the chair onto the back seat.

In the Camelot, we ordered chicken and chips – or 'chicken in the rough' as they called it, which meant that it all came in a basket and you ate it with your fingers. Mary would have a lager while I ordered two pints of Guinness and followed up with a whiskey and a cigarette (Carrolls had become my favourite, though if Mary joined me, hers was Players No 6). We felt very grown up.

'I'll get this,' I would say to Mary at the end of the night. It was important to me to pay the bill. I didn't earn much, but it was more than the peanuts Mary got as a trainee nurse.

Mary found the whole hospital set up tough. Once or twice, she had been given the job of dropping meals at the rumpus room door and she felt for two lads who seemed to always be in there. She started bringing one of them to her parents' house on her day off, just to give him a break from the hospital.

'Sure, he doesn't even know what's going on, Martin, and he's just getting more and more frustrated in there.'

I agreed with her, but if we had criticised the senior staff, there would have been hell to pay. It might have screwed things up for the other children.

One night, Mary was on night duty when a little girl passed away. The

Something about Mary

matron told her to lay the dead girl out and wheel her to the mortuary.

Children passing like that was a fairly regular occurrence.

'Sure, they are in heaven now,' the nurses said matter-of-factly, and in the morning, when the other children got up for breakfast, they were told to go into the chapel to say the Rosary and pay their respects. There was no space for any grief.

Mary just couldn't get her head around this. When she went off duty the next morning, instead of going to bed, she came looking for me.

'I have never seen a dead person before,' she sobbed.

'It happens, Mary,' I said.

I wanted to offer her some consolation, but I suppose the truth was I had become de-sensitised to the tragedy of it all.

Soon after, Mary was given the task of minding four children who had been sent down from Donegal for a week of intensive speech and language therapy.

Mary said she saw terror in the faces of these children.

'They have lived a normal life,' she told me. 'Why wouldn't they be distraught at everything that is going on here?'

Things were starting to change, though. A highly qualified new nurse called Marion arrived from Temple Street that autumn and she got the rumpus room closed down within weeks. She just said it straight, 'No, you can't be doing this,' and, fair play to her, she held her own against the older staff. She must have been willing to take it further if she'd had to.

But Mary was scarred by what she'd seen at the hospital in eight months, and when her contemporaries started getting decent trainee jobs in London, she told me she had to give it a go. What could I say?

I bought her a giant panda from the Crolly Dolly factory and gave it to

Never Know Your Place

her to take with her.

'That'll remind you of me,' I said.

At first, I thought we might survive the break. I was still able to hold a pen, so I wrote her a couple of letters. Told her the Irish Sea was breaking my heart in two, or something like that. But the excitement of London in the seventies was too much and her replies stopped coming.

Chapter 11

Baldoyle Boys

One of my jobs as the hospital's recreation manager was to give educational talks about disability at local schools to drum up volunteers. I arrived, tired and conscious that I was reeking of Carrolls, into a classroom one spring morning in 1975. The lads I was speaking to were fifth-year students at Ardscoil La Salle, Raheny, and must have been around fifteen years old.

I had just turned twenty-one, and I was still feeling burnt by Mary's departure to London. I'd grown my hair long, having concluded (based on compliments from Mary) that it was my best physical feature, and I was cultivating an unshaven and fashionably dishevelled appearance.

I saw the lads looking at me with interest. I had an electric wheelchair, bought for me by Billy McNeill (though I decided to wait till later before I told the lads that), and I took my time reversing into the teacher's spot at the head of the classroom.

I began my spiel about the practicalities of using a wheelchair, and the ice was inadvertently broken when I started explaining what happened in a session with an occupational therapist.

'One of the most useful things is learning how to screw a screwdriver,' I said, cursing my innocence the minute it came out.

Never Know Your Place

One of the lads, Niall Ó Baoill, whose face I recognised from Baldoyle United FC, muttered something under his breath. A boy they called Fluey – real name Michael Fleming – chimed in, and soon the class was in stitches.

It was obvious Niall and Fluey needed a challenge in life. When they realised I had a sense of humour and access to a swimming pool, it didn't take long to get them and their friends, John Duffy and Big Fitz down to the hospital.

The first project the De La Salle gang undertook was a twenty-four-hour soccer marathon to fund new sports equipment for us, and from then on they were part of everything we did.

Fluey was as free-spirited and wild as they come. He carried his football everywhere and couldn't get down a corridor in the hospital without knocking an arm – or worse, a head – off a statue. Conveniently, John Duffy, who regularly bunked off school to volunteer, was something of a MacGyver and he got to work quickly, gluing the statue back together, while Fluey stood there grumbling, 'Well, what are the holy statues doing there in the first place? Why can't we move them so we can play football?'

Fluey was right. I had never understood why we spent our lives weaving our wheelchairs and crutches around those cold figures.

Niall Ó Baoill was a natural leader, a nice-looking lad and an excellent footballer, going places with Baldoyle United, under the management of Kit Byrne. He had apparently known my name since he was in national school.

'You were supposed to be dead by now,' he said the first time we had a proper conversation. 'I remember when I was in fifth or sixth class, we did a Christmas toy collection for the hospital and our teacher told us about a doomed young boy called Martin Naughton who wouldn't last a year! Now

Baldoyle Boys

look at you with your electric wheelchair and facial hair!'

I didn't take offence and his irreverence set the tone for many future conversations. Born in New York, Niall carried a sense of being an outsider and he shared my yearning to feel more connected to the people around him. Above all, he was a solid person and a great communicator, who could put a spin on anything I was doing so that everybody wanted to be involved.

I noticed he could be hard on himself, but that gave him compassion for the young people in the hospital and the things they were going through.

The other key member of the De La Salle gang 'Big Fitz', or Dave Fitzgibbon, was tall, somewhat rounded, and strong enough to lift anything or anyone. His father, who was from Cork, kept a close eye on him and to Big Fitz's great embarrassment turned up at the hospital one evening to interrogate me.

'These are wonderful young men,' his dad said. 'But why do you let them smoke? Every time I look at them, they are smoking, smoking, smoking …'

I told him straight: 'I let them do whatever they want as long as they help me do what I want.'

I saw my role as offering a sort of enlightened friendship. These were young guys with a healthy appetite for life and a desire to be useful. All right, there was a bit of smoking and drinking, but most of the time they were learning and 'bettering themselves', as they say.

In return, the De La Salle lads together with a bunch of bohemian girls from Santa Sabina School in Sutton were the free labour that enabled me to take on all the tasks of putting the children to bed, relieving the hospital orderly of that duty and allowing me to keep the children up until 9pm. The Santa Sabina girls, which included Hilary Fannin and her friends Caroline Callaghan and Tina Egan, could go into the girls' ward on the first floor and

Never Know Your Place

Hospital children racing in their power wheelchairs at an event organised by Baldoyle Hospital Sports Club in 1970s. Winning was dependent on a mixture of skill and battery life.

that was crucial in getting more hospital girls down to our club.

We started hosting major competitions, such as the first national All-Ireland Under-16s Paraplegic Championships, and for less sporty children we introduced integrated Brownies and Scouts with children from the village.

For me, it had never been about sport for the sake of sport. It was about the psychological side. I was trying to change the way institutional kids thought about themselves; the way Weiss and Guttmann changed the way adults with spinal injuries felt about themselves; the way Jock Stein injected pride and ambition into his Celtic team.

My aim was deliberately to mix things up for every child. The less routine the better.

'I think we should have tea and biscuits in a different place today,' I

Baldoyle Boys

would say to the younger children. 'Where would *you* like to have your tea?'

I wanted to undo the mechanical way they had lived, to awaken their brains to the concept of choosing how and where they spent their time. To give them the idea that they could direct their own lives.

We printed tracksuits with the initials 'BHSC' across them and wearing them made us feel like members of a proper club rather than patients. The tracksuit jersey was something to be proud of, and it wasn't just disabled children who wore it – it was the village children and the volunteers too.

At competitions, we chanted our Celtic-inspired club anthem:

You won't beat me, I'm part of the Doyle
You won't beat me, I'm part of the Doyle
You won't beat me, I'm part of the Doyle
Till the day I die
Till the day I die!

Martin and young people from Baldoyle Hospital Sports Club (BHSC) taking part in the St Patrick's Day parade in Dublin.

Never Know Your Place

When we entered the St Patrick's Day parade for the first time, the De La Salle lads painted the words 'Integration' and 'Don't underrate us' in big letters on the side of our float, and our athletes did wheelies ahead of the truck to the astonishment of crowds who had never seen that sort of stuff before.

In those years, 'Naughton' morphed into 'Knockers' and the De La Salle lads never called me anything else.

My other nickname was 'the Buddha (of Baldoyle)' because if I was not in the sports hall, or keeping watch on the swimming pool, I could be found sitting cross-legged on my bed with people convened in the room

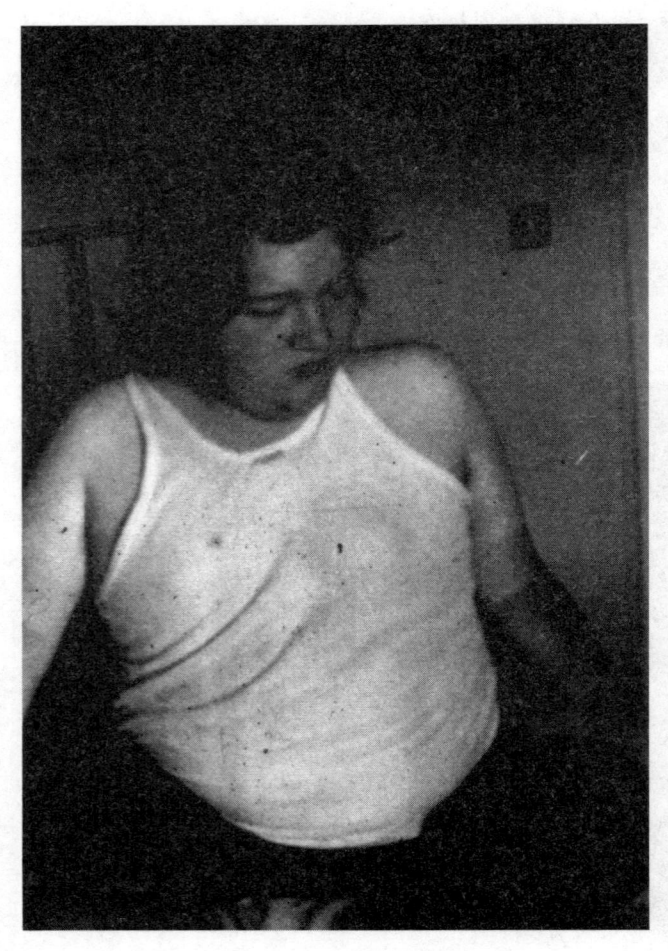

Martin, nicknamed 'the Buddha (of Baldoyle)' by some, sitting on his bed in Baldoyle Hospital. The bed doubled up as his desk and centre of operations.

Baldoyle Boys

around me. I didn't like this nickname – the physical associations weren't flattering – but I couldn't help but be touched by the nod to my quasi-mayoral position.

My bed was my desk, and the small ward I shared with six other boys was like a public office. It was close to the hospital entrance and had an internal window through which I kept watch on who was coming and going. I was not shy to call out to anyone who might be useful.

On the other end of the corridor was the smoking room which staff used for their breaks. That room was quiet in the evenings, so I commandeered it as my living area. After the activities finished, the De La Salle lads gathered around me on the upholstered smoking benches. 'Convening my night council,' I called it.

We played Bowie, Rod Stewart, Simon & Garfunkel and Cat Stevens on my record player.

'Can you put it back to "The Sound of Silence"?' I asked again and again, until the lads started to complain. Then I'd request 'Father and Son'.

We drank endless pots of tea, ate sandwiches made up by Georgie Nibbs or one of the nicer night nurses, and lit up.

'My dad said the queue outside the dole office in Gardiner Street on Thursday was worse than it's been in a while,' Big Fitz said.

'Yeah, I see that all round the town these days,' said Niall. 'In no time it will be another mass exodus to New York, Boston and elsewhere, just like in the 1950s.'

'At least ordinary people over there know how to speak up for themselves,' I said.

John Duffy nodded. 'In this country, everyone gets told where they belong, and they just accept it.'

Never Know Your Place

Some nights we could be talking politics, thinking, dreaming, coming up with plans to better the world until three in the morning.

In the daytime I felt burdened by the rigid dynamics of the institution in which I operated, but in that smoking room I felt relaxed, like my imagination could run riot.

I lived my whole life – even my sleeping hours – in a public space. But I couldn't blame the hospital authorities for this lack of privacy because it was of my own making. When I'd moved back from the Cheshire Home to start the job as recreation manager, I'd been given a room of my own – a long-disused first-floor room that had once been an isolation room for contagious diseases. It was the only room above a short corridor that linked the older convent building to the hospital.

At first it had been gratifying to be allowed up to the first floor, off-limits to all but staff and girls, but each night as I'd tried to sleep, I'd been kept awake by whispering. It had sounded to me like the hushed, secretive tones of nuns (no one else whispered quite like that). I'd put up some holy pictures, dowsed the place with a few bottles of holy water, but a few days later, I'd had a particularly bad night. When the night matron had checked on me at 2am, she'd found me sweating and struggling to get out of bed. That was it. From then on, I was keen to share a room.

Whoever those whispering nuns were, I'd thought, they'd really wanted me out.

Chapter 12

Special Treatment

Outside the hospital walls my disability was a free pass into pretty much anywhere. The endless awkwardness of the public meant I could get away with murder without being challenged. The sort of malarkey that would never work these days.

The De La Salle lads were too young to be drinking buddies, but there were two village lads I could rely on. Big Bren – real name Brendan O'Connor – was even bigger than Big Fitz of the De La Salle Gang and he lived within a hundred yards of the hospital. He was red-haired, bulky, and had a distinctive springy walk. He must have covered three feet with every step. A committed boxer and weightlifter, he was a man of few words but the first to offer to lift me up any stairs.

I hated being lifted, but nearly every pub or club in Dublin was in a Georgian building, and if it had to be done, Big Bren was the only man I trusted to do it. He was the guy who got me in and out of places.

Big Bren had started as a 'breaster' on a truck when he was fifteen – a breaster being the person who helps the driver with the loading and unloading – and since eighteen, he had been driving his own forty-foot truck around Ireland and Europe. But any time Big Bren was home, he was straight into the hospital to help out with our Scouts club.

Never Know Your Place

Martin's close friend Big Bren, second from left, with other volunteers and young people at the hospital, including Dianne Cummins (far left), at Baldoyle Hospital Sports Club in the late 1970s.

My other pal was Damien Lynch. Also a Scouts volunteer, he was a good-looking charmer, a hit with the women and frequently involved, although marriage never followed. I thought of Damien as my Public Relations Officer because he wasn't afraid to go ahead and investigate any situation – nor was he one bit behind the door when it came to asking for special treatment.

Our favourite venues were the club in Barry's Hotel just off Parnell Square, The Pig and Whistle near Constitution Hill, and The Country Club in Portmarnock. It hadn't taken Damien and Big Bren long to work out that my disability was a golden ticket. Crashing any party was easy, as was getting into any gig. If anyone had the temerity to challenge us, we just started quoting fictional disability regulations and they soon backed down.

If there was a queue into a club, I'd say loudly to Damien and Big Bren,

Special Treatment

'The man on the door is calling us, we'd better go up.'

The crowd would part politely to let us through.

When we'd get to the door, I'd say, 'The man sent for us,' and the confused and embarrassed bouncer would let us straight in.

To reach new levels of daring, to chance our arm and get into better places for less money, that was our mission in life. None of our jobs paid much, and if we wanted to have fun it had to be on the cheap.

The same modus operandi applied when we progressed to bigger adventures, like our trip to the Stoke Mandeville Games in the summer of 1975.

At Holyhead Station, I stopped the conductor and asked, 'Could you point us to first class?'

I had noticed they rarely asked for a ticket if you looked the part, and if you were disabled, they were afraid to ask.

From Holyhead, we travelled to Euston Station, where, having had a few beers along the way and no sleep, even Big Bren's strength was no match for the narrow, jerky escalator that seemed the only way to change platforms. Halfway up, Big Bren lost balance with me in his arms, and you should have seen the crowd clear behind us as he stumbled backwards, step by step. I could feel him adjusting his heavy frame to make sure he protected me by taking the impact if we hit the floor, but he regained control.

It was early morning when we made it to Aylesbury, the nearest town to Stoke Mandeville, and got the taxi from the station to our boarding house at 33 Walton Road. The landlady set out the rules before Big Bren carried me upstairs to our room. The three of us were in serious need of a kip and went out like a light.

The next thing I knew Big Bren was shaking me and Damien, and shouting, 'Quick, it's ten to nine. Breakfast ends at nine. We'll be late for the Games.'

Never Know Your Place

The lads rushed to get me downstairs, but while the table was set, there was no sign of the landlady.

'Ah no, she must have given up on us,' I said.

So we left the B&B and made our way a mile down the street to Stoke Mandeville Hospital. The sky was grey and moody, and while there were a few athletes around, there wasn't much atmosphere. I waved hello to a fresh-faced Michael Cunningham, the 'blond dynamite' from Baldoyle, who was practising javelin in a corner of the main field.

Big Bren and Damien looked exhausted and hung-over, but my head was starting to clear and I started to suspect night was actually falling. But was it half nine on Sunday night or Monday night, I wondered? I made my way over to Michael and asked him what day of the week it was. It was still Sunday. We'd only slept a few hours in the B&B. Our walk was not in vain, however, because a staff member came over to tell me that my wallet, which contained the tickets for the Games and the funds to keep the three of us going for the week, had been handed in by the taxi driver who had brought us from the station. I hadn't even noticed it was missing.

Despite our undignified start, the 1975 Stoke Mandeville Games turned out to be wonderful, and I got a real kick out of seeing people I'd grown up with in the hospital – Michael Cunningham, Kathleen Egan and Julie Cosgrove – as professional athletes on an international stage. When Kathleen was playing her table tennis final, I caught my old friend Ludwig Guttmann's eye across the stadium hall, and he gave me a thumbs-up.

We returned to Holyhead at the end of the week, travelling in the first-class carriage again – but this time a beady-eyed conductor at Euston noticed and he asked us to move.

'No problem, sir,' said Big Bren. 'I apologise for the error. But in the

Special Treatment

interests of safety, I can't risk lifting him off and on the train again, so I'll need to carry him through the carriages. Would you mind delaying our departure by just ten or fifteen minutes so I can sort this out? It really wouldn't be safe to carry him while we are moving.'

The conductor looked at his timetable and muttered something about 'next time' as he walked away.

*　*　*

The following year the three of us decided we were ready for our biggest adventure yet, the Toronto Paralympics followed by a proper road trip, the kind we'd seen in the movies.

At Shannon Airport there was widespread chaos as Aer Lingus staff tried to work out how to get me on board the plane. Rather than block up the passenger walkway to the front of the plane while Big Bren carried me, they decided it was better for two of their skinny, inexperienced officials to lift me up the rear stairs. I did not fancy being part of this dangerous experiment, so I began acting very officially, mustering my best authoritarian tone and referring to a 'committee' in Dublin that had great expertise in the areas of wheelchair access and safety and would not approve of this method.

'You should send a man to Dublin to be trained by this committee,' I offered.

Now of course, in 1976 such a committee was a complete work of fiction (these days it might actually exist), but it had the desired effect.

'A com-mit-tae?' the Aer Lingus official said slowly in his west of Ireland accent.

Yes, a 'com-mit-tae,' I repeated, stone-faced but aping his accent, as others had once aped mine.

Never Know Your Place

By this stage Big Bren was falling about laughing behind me, but the seed of doubt had been planted, and they let Big Bren carry me up the front steps.

At the Games, Barbara's friend Julie Cosgrove won the first Gold in table tennis, and Michael Cunningham later won Gold and set a world record in javelin. We all stayed in college accommodation at York University, and in the evenings, we hung out with gangs of athletes, including a new Irish athlete called Paddy McCool, who had won Silver in discus and club throw. A member of the British team drove us from pub to pub, and if McCool, who was an accomplished musician, sang, we usually ended up with free beer.

Strangers in pubs often asked how I ended up in the wheelchair, and Big Bren and I entertained ourselves by telling a story we'd been using for a while.

'We were wrestling buddies,' I'd say, poker-faced.

'We were the best of mates,' Bren would add, 'but didn't I go and break his bloody back when we were training and now I feel so bad I have to look after him for the rest of his life.'

There was a few seconds' silence as they looked us over, but Bren being such a big lad and me being not so slim myself, you could see they thought it plausible. Not knowing what to say, they usually headed straight up to the bar to buy us another drink.

Once the Games were over, Big Bren, Damien and I drove around Eastern Canada and New England for two weeks in a rental. I could have been vulnerable – a young guy in a wheelchair far from home – but I never felt that way. Big Bren helped me with practical tasks, but compared with him I was streetwise, and he looked to me for guidance. When the money ran

Special Treatment

out and we had to return the car, we hitchhiked. This usually ended up with nice couples stopping for us, and Big Bren lifting me into the passenger seat beside the driver (in those days it was inevitably the man) while he and Damien – the two burly charmers – squeezed into the back with an embarrassed woman.

There was a bank strike in Ireland that summer and when our funds ran low it was impossible to get money sent over. The cheapest places to stay were campsites in the First Nation reservations around Toronto, so that was where we headed for the final two weeks.

Now there was a group of people who were living like second-class citizens. Their heads hung low as they boarded the buses outside the reservation. As I talked to them over bowls of stew and cornbread in the makeshift restaurant, they constantly referred back to the history of their people, as if the past was all that gave them a sense of dignity. Most of the time, they seemed defeated by society, with no hope, no vision of how things might get better. It wasn't my battle to fight, but I felt for them.

Only their traditional chanting seemed to lift their spirits. I loved lying in my tent listening to it. As the days went by, I learnt some of the chants. (I still use some of them today when I'm under pressure.)

As I had expected, there was lots of alcohol in the reservation, and it was true what people said; they couldn't hold their drink. Thursday was the liveliest night of the week, because Thursday was dole day in the reservation – just as it was back in Dublin. It seemed a symbolic reminder that downtrodden people are the same the world over.

Chapter 13

Bringing Home the Bacon

I began the eighties in a bullish frame of mind. It may have been a bleak time economically, but it was the start of the Haughey era and North-East Dublin was a strategic place to be. The workings of local, and even national, politics were starting to seem within my grasp. If there was any little bit of money going, we heard about it first.

Michael Woods was our TD in Dublin North-East and he made a point of calling to me in the hospital sports hall one afternoon.

'I want you to know my door is always open,' he said. It was clear he considered me a community force worth courting.

'I've heard about what you are doing in the hospital and in the village, Martin,' he continued, 'and I am a big supporter of Baldoyle FC.'

As a result of our work, Baldoyle had already become the first place in the country to get a paid youth officer, a local lad in his twenties called Michael Dawson. Michael was affable, but also had palpable ambition and a nose for politics. He'd joined Fianna Fáil and was rising up the party ranks.

With the help of Niall Ó Baoill and the De La Salle lads, Michael and I were overseeing the construction of an integrated youth centre for the village, and we'd even convinced the council to ramp the pavements so

Bringing Home the Bacon

young people in wheelchairs could get between the hospital and the youth centre. It must have made Baldoyle the most wheelchair-accessible place in Ireland.

In less than a decade, I had gone from having a vague plan around sport to a situation where the generation coming of age in the hospital had local friends, and dreams and expectations for their future, albeit modest ones.

In 1981, for the first time, two teenagers, Paddy Cullen and Michael Weblin, both physically very able but nevertheless wheelchair users, left Baldoyle Hospital and moved straight into a local authority house to live independently. That had never happened before.

And a few of the most physically capable people of my generation had escaped the Cheshire Home.

Barbara, who still had much greater mobility than me, had found a clerical job and was living with her friend Julie.

Kathleen had got married (she was now Kathleen Reynolds) and had just given birth to her second son.

'I now have a family to call my own,' Kathleen told me when I rang to congratulate her. 'With my first son, I had to put up with a few raised eyebrows, but this time around everyone knows I'm well able!'

* * *

The year 1981 was declared the first 'United Nations International Year of Disabled Persons', and the publicity talking about 'equalisation of opportunities' and 'a wheelchair in every home' seemed to mirror the new identity we had forged for ourselves.

But there was a group of young people we were in danger of leaving behind. These were the children who had the greatest physical challenges, and many had intellectual disabilities as well.

Never Know Your Place

Some of them were housed in a special unit on the first floor of the hospital, in an area not easily accessible to other children, and their lives felt segregated and medicalised. They had benefitted least from our work in the sports club, so when Dermot Mooney and I set up a fundraising committee to capitalise on the public goodwill associated with the Year, those kids had to be the focus.

There wasn't much we could do to change their daily lives, but we came up with a plan to send thirty of them on holiday in the Algarve with local families. That way, the children would experience a normal family holiday, away from an institutional environment and with other children who had been on holiday before – children who understood that a holiday was about serious fun.

Dermot invited a local businessman, Jimmy Connolly, to join our fundraising committee. Jimmy, soon known to me as 'JC', was a force to be reckoned with. In his mid-forties, he was a Malahide-based entrepreneur, but also a family man who liked to look out for the younger generation.

To pull the holiday project off, we needed more than £30,000, which was a sizeable sum. I remember thinking, 'I could buy three good houses for that.'

But it didn't faze JC as he sold tickets for a string of fundraising events.

'Don't you worry,' he said to me. 'I'll bring home the bacon. You just mind it and keep the place in order.'

I remember there was one boy who needed a particularly high level of support. Including him was going to be very expensive.

Questions were asked at the committee meeting. 'Is it really realistic for a boy like that to go on holiday? Is he not too disabled?'

Even I had started to hesitate.

Bringing Home the Bacon

Martin at the presentation of a fundraising car draw, probably in the early 1980s.

But JC couldn't accept this boy was 'too disabled' to enjoy a holiday. Within days, he had found the extra thousands.

It turned out to be a lesson to us all on the importance of making decisions around individuals rather than money, because that boy benefitted more than anyone from his trip to the Algarve that summer. His life didn't turn out to be very long, but in the few years that followed, he talked more about that holiday than anything else, and when he spoke what was evident was not just the fun he'd had, but his pride that others had seen fit to give him such an opportunity.

During that project JC and I discovered we made a good team.

'When all of this is over, we'll have to work together in business,' he said. 'We have to make money.'

Never Know Your Place

This was a new experience for me. I'd fought so hard to be recognised in Baldoyle Hospital as a person with a professional value, and now here was a real businessman telling me that my skills had commercial value. The world must be moving on, I thought. It felt good.

I let JC's job offer sit at the back of my mind for a few months. Any change had to be done carefully. The hospital was not just my employer, it was my home. But I kept asking myself, 'Do I really want to live in an institution – even if it is on my terms?'

The De La Salle boys were starting to move on to other things in life, coming into the hospital less often. Big Bren was engaged to a girl who worked in the hospital kitchens and John Duffy was going steady with one of the trainee nurses. The friendships would always be there, but I knew I wouldn't be able to hold my old gang together much longer.

That Christmas, I sat down with a core group of friends, including Niall Ó Baoill, Big Bren, John Duffy and Michael Dawson, and I told them about my idea.[5]

'I want to go solo,' I said.

'I'm going to need to set up a rota and have somebody with me 24/7 – and it's all on a voluntary basis. I need you to be there for the good and the bad, the fun stuff and the hard stuff.'

Were they up to it?

'Yes,' they all said, without question they would help me. I would be their new project.

Looking back, I may have been the nominated leader, but the years I had spent with those guys had challenged me, pushed me on. Before I'd met them, my sole goal in life had been to make a life for myself in the hospital, where I felt safe and comfortable, but those lads had helped me

Bringing Home the Bacon

think bigger. They had helped me realise I could survive outside the walls of an institution. After all, on our holidays and nights out there hadn't been a nurse in sight.

'We'll never see you stuck, Martin,' the lads used to say.

I might have been the guy who brought those lads together, but it was they who set me free.

Chapter 14

The Real World

I remember January 1982 well. The snow was so heavy Michael Dawson put chains on his blue Renault 4 to bring me to view the houses and flats available to rent. It was the usual story – stairs and narrow doorways.

Then we heard of a bungalow beside a grocer's shop, 33a Baldoyle Road. It turned out to be shabby but workable. Michael, Big Bren and the lads from BHSC got to work straightaway, painting the inside of the house, installing wooden ramps at the front and back doors.

I moved out of the hospital in April.

Leaving an institution is not an easy thing to do. There were many who asked, 'How is Martin going to manage?'

After all, the only part of my body that really worked was my mouth. I could eat and talk for Ireland, but my legs were useless and my arms were getting weaker. I was going to need somebody to help me with just about everything.

But the guys were true to their word. My bungalow became the new hub for the comings and goings of the gang, plus any younger siblings they could rope in. We divided the day into shifts and one of them was always there, following my instructions, helping me transfer in or out of my wheelchair, get in or out of bed, sit up, undress, wash, or go to the toilet.

The Real World

Nighttime was the most demanding shift, because I got uncomfortable and needed to be turned – an hour would rarely pass without me calling for assistance.

Often the lads would bring down a cheese sandwich or something their mam had cooked. They knew food was the way to my heart. He who brought the best sandwich – or better still, a piece of meat – would get the most out of me. That might mean driving lessons in the banger of a van I'd bought, help with their Leaving Cert Irish, or a few Carrolls.

Nonetheless, there were times when there were gaps in cover and the

Martin, probably taken in the year before he left Baldoyle Hospital.

Never Know Your Place

reality of living independently had to be faced. One Saturday night, my friend Hubert McCormack, who was now eighteen and in his final year at Baldoyle Hospital, was looking for a bed for a night. His brother had driven him back from the family home in Longford at the end of the holidays, and they wanted to go out to some live music in Dublin and delay going back into the hospital for one more precious night.

'Sure, you can both stay here, Hubie,' I said without any thought. 'I've a spare bed.'

In the morning, Hubert's brother got him up before heading off back to Longford, and one of the lads, Big Bren I think it was, got me up. After they left, Hubert and I settled in to watch *The Blues Brothers* on VHS.

As the day wore on, we both started thinking we'd love a bite to eat, and I realised I hadn't anyone coming until the evening.

'I am pretty sure there's a French stick in the fridge,' I said.

'That'd be lovely, Martin,' Hubert said. 'But how are we going to get it out?'

Hubert and I had a very similar disability, but at the time I had the advantage of being in a power wheelchair, whereas Hubert only had a manual one, so I went at it in the kitchen. It took me nearly an hour – all the time with Hubert singing away in his fine baritone in the background – but I got the fridge door open and the bread out and onto the kitchen table. Somehow I even got a lump of butter on the top of the crust.

But there was no way I could split the bread in two.

'You bite into one end, and I'll bite the other,' I said to Hubert, and we went at the French stick as if we were wrestling over a bone.

Hubert and I laughed about that day many times afterwards. We had to laugh. And it was true that the joy I felt at my new freedom far

The Real World

Martin's friend Hubert McCormack (second from right), aged around seventeen, with a group of young men at Baldoyle Hospital Sports Club. On the left is Sean Wynne and Pat Thompson. To Hubert's right is Colm Sherry.

outweighed the inconveniences and risks.

After a few months, I was ready to take the next step.

When I'd got the job in the hospital eight years earlier, my mother had apparently said to my sisters, 'Sure, he won't keep it, he'll want something else!'

It turned out she knew me well.

I handed in my notice that June, resigning from my job as recreation manager and all my additional voluntary roles. It had to be a clean break because there was another new head nun taking over and I sensed she and I would not get along. She seemed keen to go back to the medical model, with tight restrictions on people coming and going. I couldn't fight that fight again.

Never Know Your Place

When the Reverend Mother who presided over the whole of the Convent Community heard I was leaving, she made a point of pulling me aside.

'Now, Martin, as you go out on your big adventure, I want to assure you that I'll make sure your post is kept open for a few months. You just come to me and let me know if you have a change of mind.'

That might sound generous, but I was hurt. What she was really saying was that she expected me to fail in the real world.

Fortunately, I had JC's relentless positivity to buoy me up. Straightaway he gave me the job of managing some of his property in Kinsealy – two industrial units and a parking yard. The first thing I had to do was rent out one of the units, and in the second unit he told me to set up a signwriting, crash repair and car servicing business, which we called 'Allstar'.

Now, all I knew about cars was that they came in different colours, but JC wasn't concerned. 'Find decent people to work for you and learn the rest as you go,' he told me.

JC was a wheeler and dealer. As well as Allstar, he had a factory maintenance business and a building company. He was eager to teach me about business.

'Don't you go off waffling on paper,' he said, keen to knock any bad practices I'd picked up in the hospital out of me. 'Policies are a waste of time.'

When I started hiring lads to work in the garage, his advice was simple: 'Just get them to agree that they'll show up on time, won't leave before their time, and that they'll do a little bit of work in between.'

JC said the rest would come from the culture of the place, which they'd soon pick up once they were in the door.

His advice on sales pitches was similarly matter-of-fact: 'Just show them that you can do it, have done it before, and that they'd be mad not to let

The Real World

you do it for them. You've got ten minutes to make your impression – after that, forget it.'

I learnt fast. When a car pulled up, I'd call, 'Come on over here and open the bonnet,' to one of the lads. I'd peer in carefully, pausing here and there, and then issue instructions.

'Take out that spark plug!'

'Show me the alternator!'

The lads were my hands and my job was to inspire confidence. It was like when I'd taught swimming in the hospital. No one had ever dared say, 'But you can't swim!' and now no one dared say, 'But you can't fix an engine!'

JC may have talked a lot about the bottom line, but if he ever had to step in to take me to the bathroom or lift me up steps, he did it without fuss. He was determined to ensure I didn't fail and took pleasure in seeing me grow.

On one occasion, Michael Dawson leaned on me, as I had leaned on him many times before, for help with a local lad, Robby Martin, who was in trouble with the law. Robby was accused of attempted car theft and unless someone was willing to post a bond and vouch for him going forward, he was going down. I asked JC if there was anything he could do and he went straight down to Howth Garda Station to talk to Robby.

Later that day, JC walked into the garage.

'You are right, Martin,' he said. 'I've spoken to the lad, and I don't think we can let him swing for it.'

He had posted the £500 bond out of his own pocket.

Once free, Robby was sent down to Allstar to start working off his debt. I had him steam-clean the inside of ambulances (the worst of all jobs) for fifteen days straight. I thought that would get rid of him, but it didn't. He kept going without complaint.

Never Know Your Place

Robby was a huge punk rocker – I used to marvel at the number of safety pins in his ears – but he turned out to be the hardest worker. Once I had the means, I felt it was only fair to reduce my demands on the BHSC volunteers, and in 1983, Robby became my first paid assistant. He came in to get me up in the mornings and did long shifts, supporting me at work in Allstar, and in the evening at home (which by 1983 was a ground-floor corporation flat on Baldoyle Road – cramped but more affordable than the bungalow). The only downside was Robby's taste for deafening rock music, but I chose to close my ears and enjoy his company, and I'm glad I did.

If I asked Robby to work late on a Saturday, he'd say, 'That's all right, gaffer,' and ask if he could nip home and change so that when he clocked off he'd be ready for a night out in his ripped jeans and safety-pin attire.

I didn't realise at the time but what Robby and I had – that respectful and warm, but at the same time professional relationship – was the model that would later enable thousands of Irish disabled people to live independently. I was just grateful that JC and Robby had shown up when they did. It amazes me how often people seem to come into my life not a minute too soon and not a minute too late.

Chapter 15

The Hat

Mary was back in Dublin. She was working in a GP surgery in Fairview and a mutual friend had met her there. She wrote her new phone number on a scrap of paper and asked him to give it to me.

I rang her straightaway and we arranged to meet up at the Dollymount House on the Clontarf Road after work.

It was early autumn, and though it was not yet 7pm, it was dark when Robby parked the van and put down the ramp to get me out. I had come early to avoid making a fuss of my arrival.

I chose a table down the back but with a good view of the double doors, and Robby sat down beside me. I was wearing a black cape and a fisherman's fedora with two little feathers in it. I thought it was daring enough to be fashionable.

Mary caught my eye as she opened the door. She was wearing faded blue jeans and a darker denim jacket covered in badges and embroidery. She had white basketball runners and her hair bobbed on her shoulders as she walked towards me.

'What's with the hat, Martin?' she asked as she put her handbag on the bench and sat down.

I told her the truth. 'The hair's getting a little thinner, Mary.'

Never Know Your Place

Mary Llewellyn in the 1980s when she returned to Dublin from London.

'Aw Martin, your gorgeous black hair,' she said, not hiding her disappointment.

I left the hat on as she looked at me.

'Well, I'm getting used to the hat. It's a bit mad, but it's growing on me. Yeah, I do like it,' she said.

'It's also a visual thing,' I said. 'I like that people say, "Look at yer man in the hat and the cape" rather than "Look at yer man in the wheelchair".'

We had both changed in so many ways. She was a single mum with a young son. I was living on my own and had nothing to do with Baldoyle Hospital anymore. And my arm strength had reduced to the point that I had to have an assistant with me. But these changes were small things

The Hat

really because we were the same people. We still struggled to get a word in edgeways over each other's chatter. We still talked incessantly about music and football. It was still a lager for her and a Guinness for me.

It turned out we'd both just given up cigarettes. Not for the first (or last) time.

'Shocking,' we said in tandem and laughed.

'Did you hear Kit was robbed?' I asked her. I had banned people from telling me about the goings-on at the hospital, but Hubert had rightly made an exception the week before.

Mary shook her head.

'He was attacked getting out of his car in the hospital car park. He had just come back from the Bank of Ireland in Sutton with the weekly staff wages. The guy must have been waiting for him. Nobody saw what happened. One of the maintenance staff found him lying unconscious. And he had the handle of the leather briefcase in his right hand.'

Mary was disgusted. 'Ah, bless him. Is he alright now?'

'He still has some bruises. The guy hit him a few times and he was a bit shook afterwards, but he's alright now. He was back training the Baldoyle FC youth team on Thursday.'

'That's Kit, though,' Mary said. 'The handle in his hand. He wouldn't let his people be robbed without putting up a fight.'

'I know. That man has the keenest sense of right and wrong.'

Mary glanced over at Robby, unsure of whether to include him in the conversation. I nodded to Robby and he leaned over the table to lift my Guinness to my mouth.

'Your arms have got weaker, Martin?' Mary said.

'They have. You know how it goes.'

Never Know Your Place

I didn't know what else to say about it, so I started repeating what the consultant had told me. 'If you think of the muscles as light bulbs and the nerves as wiring, all the bulbs are in great shape. It's just the power supply getting to them is less each year.'

Mary took another sip of her drink and leaned across the table to lift my pint for me.

'No, Mary,' I said. 'Let Robby do that. That's what he's here for. You are my friend, not my assistant.'

It went against Mary's nature not to help, but I needed this boundary if she was coming back into my life.

'How are you managing with meals? Are the lads cooking for you?' she asked. Mary knew I loved my meat and two veg, and she knew I liked it done right.

'They do their best,' I said. 'The good news is I get bacon these days. Sometimes the lads boil the bejasus out of the cabbage though. And the cheese sauce they put on the cauliflower is very watery.'

'Ah no, and I bet they chop the carrots in rings?'

'Always,' I said.

'Aw God, Martin, if I let you do everything else your way, can you at least let me teach them a thing or two?'

I hoped after that night we might pick up again where we had left off. And there were times when it nearly happened. But it was Catholic Ireland and it wasn't easy for anyone, let alone disabled people, to talk about the complications that relationships involve. So, we kept putting it aside, instead weaving in and out of each other's lives in the years that followed as the closest of friends, the kind that might go quiet for a month or two but will suddenly turn up when you need them most.

Chapter 16

Dreams and Regrets

In 1987 JC and I sold the Allstar business and site as a going concern. JC thought it was the right time to review his investments. Residential property prices were low but with his business nose he could smell an upturn. He even sold his house and moved into a creepy old convent in Malahide with grounds and development potential.

JC wanted to be in a position to act when the time was right. We shared a belief in the importance of timing, the need to be a step ahead of the crowd – though my instincts were more about social change than economics. As the first signs of economic recovery appeared, I kept urging JC to sell the convent.

'Liquidise now, before it's too late!'

'No, no, no,' he'd say, shaking his head. (He held his nerve until the nineties, and he turned out to be right.)

I learnt a lot about business from JC – enough to know that, while it wasn't my true calling in life, I had the basic skills to run any sort of set-up.

With a few quid from the sale of Allstar in my pocket, I decided to take a few months to consider my options and spend a long holiday with my sister Chris in Boston.

Chris had started her American life in Dorchester, which everyone

Never Know Your Place

said was a suburb of Boston but the capital of Connemara, and had then moved with her husband Noel and their children to Pembroke, just south of Boston. They had a quintessential American clapboard house with a porch, albeit without a picket fence. The only part that had level access was the basement, so that became my den. Set up as a bar and TV room, it suited me well, but there was no way Chris would let me eat down there. A proper sit-down dinner was a family tradition, so it was all hands on wheels once a day to push me up the steep scaffolding boards on the steps to her front door.

I took to wearing a flat tweed cap that summer – the kind my father used to wear – and as Chris's teenage sons and daughters took care of me and showed me around Boston, I allowed them to call me 'Uncle', something I'd resisted for years on the grounds of being too young.

It was easy to feel at home. So many people from Spiddal were living over there. My father's older brothers, and my mother's sister, whose husband Marty Walsh was now a big property developer, and various children and grandchildren. A crowd gathered at Chris's place one night and a few of them got talking about how jobs were so plentiful in Boston that employers like Marty and his brothers Pat and John were relying on Irish J1ers to keep them in business through the summer.

I wasn't listening for nothing.

'I know a load of young guys – all of them great workers – who'd love to come over,' I interrupted, thinking of all the unemployed lads I knew in Baldoyle.

A week later, I linked up with a second-generation Irish guy and we set up a company that organised J1 visas and work placements for Irish people.[6] His role was to line up the jobs with the employers, including the

Dreams and Regrets

Walshes, and when I headed back to Dublin I took care of the Irish end – recruiting potential J1ers, preparing CVs and submitting visa applications. Between my contacts in Baldoyle and in Spiddal, it was easy pickings.

At the start of the next J1 season, I flew back to Boston to be on hand for the summer. My first task was to give a pep talk to an audience of employers and host families. It was an occasion that benefitted from an element of showmanship, and once the Americans got over their surprise at being greeted by a guy in a hat and wheelchair, I had them open-mouthed again as they listened to my three-part guide to young Irish people.

'Irish kids are different from American kids,' I began. 'They are all drinkers and most of them are smokers.'

'In fact, most of them have been drinking from a very young age,' I added and then paused. 'But the good news is, they are well able to handle it.'

Gasps of 'Oh my goodness' could be heard from the wholesome audience.

'Secondly, cursing is normal, standard language in Ireland. It is not intended to cause offence.'

I could see them struggling to imagine what could be next and there was visible relief when I added, 'Finally, very few Irish kids can drive. Over here, it may be normal to throw the keys at anyone and expect them to get behind the wheel. Don't do that! Out of embarrassment, an Irish kid will give it a try.'

I got a kick out of the Americans, their particular brand of innocent positivity, their 'can-do' attitude to everything that came their way. They liked that I wasn't what they expected.

In America wanting more for yourself was encouraged and earned you respect. All I'd heard all my life was, 'You can't do this, you can't do that.'

Never Know Your Place

Here was a true antidote to that, something totally un-Irish.

Yes, America was a place where everything was bigger, better, fresher. A place that had produced heroes like Bobby Kennedy and Martin Luther King. Surely, such a place had to be a natural home for my way of thinking?

By the end of the 1980s, my life was lived in a kind of halfway state between America and Ireland, and I was wondering if it might make sense to move across for good. But as with all these decisions in life, there is a push and pull. My mother had died suddenly of a diabetes-related heart attack, and it made me sad to think of leaving my father in his old age. Would it be fair for me to head off across the world?

My sisters saw my dilemma. Barbara lived a quiet and private life, quite unlike mine, but we had continued our childhood habit of checking in with each other every day, and when we spoke on the phone (always in Irish), she gently reminded me of the practicalities of such a big transition, while still encouraging me to follow my heart.

But it was my eldest sister Maureen who really understood the draw of America, because she had felt it herself. She'd had a visa refusal when she was in her early twenties, and I suspected it had been her biggest disappointment.

'I saw myself doing well in America,' she said when I asked her about it. 'I would have made a different kind of life.'

Maureen was fifty now and still working as the postmistress of Spiddal. With my mother gone, I valued her role as a second mother even more, and I went to Spiddal to see her and my father as often as I could. Robby, Big Bren, or one of the other lads drove the van, but I'd had the passenger seat removed so I could see the road from my position in the back. Back-seat driving was one of my favourite pastimes and I liked to call out orders

Dreams and Regrets

Martin's sister Maureen Naughton, who was like a second mother to Martin and provided 'a positive example of how to live with a disability'.

about which route to take.

'Put your foot down!' I'd shout from the back if I thought they were going too slow, leaning my body weight forward in my wheelchair when I thought it might help get the old van going.

Once we were over halfway to Spiddal, we'd stop at a petrol station, and I would call Maureen to let her know how long we'd be. Before I hung up, Maureen always reminded me, 'Old cars round the back, Martin.'

Maureen considered herself too posh for old cars – or worse, old vans – and she didn't like them parked in her drive.

After Mikey, the original postmaster, had died, the post office had moved from its position up on the hill down into the centre of the village. That had made life easier for Maureen in some ways because she walked with difficulty.

'The hardest piece of work each day used to be getting up that hill,' she said when we talked about the old days.

She didn't mention Mikey much, but I think she missed him. They had worked so closely together, known each other's antics inside out. Everyone said they had been like an old married couple.

I knew that not long before Mikey had died, he'd made Maureen, or 'Maura' as he had called her, an offer.

'Marry me, Maura – I'll make you a wife and a widow before the year ends – and we won't even have to share a bed.'

He'd said he wanted her to have the post office and the land. Every morning, he'd ask her, 'Did you think about it, Maura?'

We'd been half hoping she would accept (if there were spoils to be had, Maureen would have been generous enough to share them), but she hadn't, and so here she was, working for the new owners in their shop in the village.

Maureen still worked six days a week – though it was a half day on Monday. She had a kind of honorary place in Spiddal village because the nature of her work meant she knew details about people's lives and had reason to go in and out of their houses.

If my brother Pádraic saw her coming out of one house or another, he'd say, 'What dragged you up there?'

She'd respond, 'I had to go.'

She didn't tell him anything more and that killed him.

And it was worse because if she was asked, as she often was, to help organise something in the village, like giving someone a lift to a doctor's appointment, she'd say, 'Surely' and then give Pádraic his orders.

Dreams and Regrets

Pádraic would go quiet for a few seconds and then mutter, 'Are you joking? Not a chance.'

The next day, you'd see him doing it.

Maureen knew how to hold her own. She had taken care of herself since her twenties, and she'd built herself a house, calling in favours and reading every page of her trusty *A-Z of Building Work*.

The people of Spiddal relied on Maureen, but it might have surprised them to know she felt she never really belonged anywhere. She was still booking tickets for Spiddal émigrés and for the family members she encouraged to visit them. She'd even convinced my parents to go to Boston a few years before my mother died. Maureen liked to get people to do things they'd otherwise never have done.

Since my mother's passing, Maureen did a lot for my father. He was getting frail but was always pleased to see me and hear about my plans.

'Keep your fingers in a few pies, Martin, if you can because you never know when there'll be a downturn,' he told me one evening, pausing to puff his pipe. 'When the tide goes out in America, everything goes out with it. There's no such thing as redundancy or benefits or so I read in the paper.'

Spiddal seemed to bring me closer to America because there was inevitably someone visiting. Each visitor would entertain us with tales of our relations, and photos from the latest weddings. As we sat before the fire, the men spoke about their work on the big construction sites, using the fire poker to draw pictures of the skyscrapers of New York, Boston and Chicago in the ashes.

If we weren't talking of America, we talked of Maureen's latest pilgrimage – Lourdes, Padre Pio, whatever. There was not a place in Italy Maureen hadn't been in the name of some saint or other. It wasn't faith that drove

Never Know Your Place

Martin in the family home in Spiddal in the late 1980s.

her; it was the entertainment, the pleasure.

The only regret Maureen ever spoke of was not intervening in my parents' decision to send Barbara and me to Baldoyle.

'I should have challenged Mam and Dad,' she told me more than once.

She said there had been talk of sending her to an institution when she was thirteen or fourteen, but she'd made a big fuss and refused to go. She'd fought her corner, she said, but not ours.

That was the past though, and Maureen was a person who believed in the future. She buried her regrets, seeing no purpose in them, and she took pleasure in other people's dreams – especially when those dreams, like mine, revolved around America.

Chapter 17

Independent State of Mind

I may never have made it to the small downtown office of the Boston Center for Independent Living if someone hadn't told me it was the only place to get a wheelchair-accessible ticket to a Red Sox game at Fenway Park. It was on my summer trip to the US in 1989. Disability was not high on my agenda at the time. I'd done that. Now I was on another path, my ears open for business opportunities to supplement my J1 work and make a permanent move to the US feasible – like whether there was more money to be made out of crash repairs, selling pizza or supplying building labour.

I arrived to find two or three staff members – all wheelchair users – busy offering advice on the phones. The guy in charge of the Red Sox tickets had a severe physical disability and speech difficulties, and I found myself directing my questions to his able-bodied assistant.

'How can somebody like this be in charge of something as important as Red Sox tickets?' I thought. I was still under the illusion that I was the only disabled person in the world who could get things done.

The Red Sox ticket guy picked up on my attitude and must have decided

Never Know Your Place

I needed my eyes opening. Before he handed me the tickets, he got me to agree to come back later that week for what he called a 'Friday afternoon session'.

The Red Sox game turned out to be a memorable one, though not for the right reasons. I went with a huge gang, including Chris and her family, but just as the game got tense, a mosquito decided he liked me and started buzzing around my head. My arms were too weak to swat it and when I tried to get help, everyone was shouting and so excited by the game that they didn't understand. So it was me versus buzzing insect, a situation which happened every now and again and reminded me of my disability like no other. Each time the creature landed, I tried with huge difficulty to slap it. It felt like hours, but I got the blasted thing in the end and let out a huge 'yeah' just as our team scored.

The following Friday when I told the guys at the Center for Independent Living about the Red Sox mosquito, they knew just what I was talking about.

'Been there, buddy,' one of them said and handed me a beer.

I'd gone back dutifully, expecting some kind of dull committee meeting, and had been surprised to find a laid-back gathering of local disabled people that rolled on into the evening. It was partly social and partly information-sharing, or 'peer consultancy' as they called it.

After that, I became a Friday regular, though my initial motivation was selfish. While the locals were 'shooting the breeze' or 'talking about issues', as they liked to say, I never lost sight of the fact that all this insider information would help me get myself set up in the US when I was ready to make the move. I was going to need to know how things worked when it came to medical care, parking badges and housing.

Independent State of Mind

As the weeks went by and I got answers to my questions, my mind was blown by how progressive America was when it came to disability. I went to see a vehicle supplier and was offered a test drive in the most technically advanced adapted van I'd ever seen. And when I enquired about housing, I was astonished to find that not only was wheelchair-accessible housing available, but rent was fixed at thirty percent of a person's income. I also heard that any disabled person who had been offered institutional accommodation automatically had the option of choosing independent accessible housing instead.

This right to independent accommodation would have been meaningless if it hadn't been backed up by a ground-breaking Personal Care Attendant (PCA) programme. Each disabled person received a grant to pay for Personal Care Attendants to support them in living in their own homes and in working. Often arrangements were made so that these PCAs could stay overnight in a second bedroom, providing twenty-four-hour support. And there was no big charity or Government department co-ordinating it all. Instead, it was the responsibility of each individual disabled person to organise their rotas, to hire and fire. I couldn't believe what I was hearing.

'This is exactly what I've been doing anyway,' I started telling everyone. 'Robby, Big Bren, all the other lads. They are my PCAs. The only difference is that in Ireland I am asking favours and paying for it all myself.'

My living arrangements may have been ahead of my time, but in other areas my attitudes lagged way behind. The guys at Boston Center for Independent Living didn't shame me by pointing out my failings. They just began gently indoctrinating me with the powerful philosophy of the American Independent Living movement. It had all started, they explained, in

Never Know Your Place

the 1970s in Berkeley, California, with a bunch of young disabled people who were sick of being treated like patients.

At the Friday night sessions, the Boston crew challenged me to re-evaluate how I saw myself as a person with a disability. Why did I feel like I had to solve every problem? Did I see success in terms of becoming more like an 'able-bodied' person, and if my aim in life was to be as able-bodied as possible, was I not setting myself up for failure?

They introduced me to the concept that my disability wasn't the cause of every problem in my life. If I couldn't get on a bus, was it because of my disability, or was it because the bus was badly designed? If I couldn't get into a building, was it because of my wheelchair, or because of the steps some architect had thoughtlessly put there? And, if I couldn't get a job easily, was it because I lacked ability, or was it because everything, from the education system to building design, was loaded against me?

Their questions stacked up and, slowly, I began to see things from a fresh perspective, to realise that I wasn't responsible for the shortcomings of society, that it was fair to expect more. I had become so single-minded about making money to fund my independence that I hadn't drawn breath to ask what sort of supports the State should provide for people like me. They reminded me of a lesson from my Baldoyle Hospital years that I had somehow forgotten: before we can change the world around us, we must first change how we see ourselves.

The people at Boston Center for Independent Living also spoke about how important it was to be proud of ourselves as disabled people. Their ethos was all about taking ownership of our lives, and never letting ourselves feel passive or dependent. There was no weakness or shame in requiring practical support, and we didn't need other people telling us how to organise that support.

'Forget the old saying, "Doctor knows best",' they joked. 'We are thinking individuals who make decisions about our own lives.'

Their motto was, 'To boldly go where everyone else has gone before.'

Hearing people talk in these terms was a bolt out of heaven.

Chapter 18

Throwing out the Rule Book

'In Ireland, if you manage to get out of an institution, you have to rely on the goodwill of your friends or family – and it doesn't matter how good they are, you have to be grateful for it.'

It was early 1991 and I was talking to a big meeting of disabled people, along with a few non-disabled supporters, around a long table in a library room belonging to the Irish Wheelchair Association in Clontarf.[7]

'In America, you can be free from this endless sense of dependency, of indebtedness,' I added.

Most of the disabled people at the meeting were living in institutions; a couple lived at home with their parents. They'd all had to ask for permission or support in various ways to get to the meeting and they were there because they wanted to be more independent.

I continued, 'If we had the sort of support they have over there, we could live, work, get on with life the way other people do.'

I had skipped my summer trip to America in 1990 to save money (besides, it wouldn't have been the same watching the World Cup over there). My J1

Throwing out the Rule Book

business income had dropped due to a downturn in the US economy, but I was still set on making the move. The Morrison Visa programme had been announced and everyone knew I would be applying. (Even the fact that the Morrison was open to disabled people seemed proof they thought disabled people could contribute to society.)

While I waited on the bureaucratic cogs to turn on the Morrison, I was spreading the ideas I'd picked up in Boston to other people who, like me, had the kind of significant disabilities that were considered a barrier to living outside an institution. One of the people at the meeting was my friend from Baldoyle Hospital, Hubert McCormack. He was now nearly thirty and living in a Cheshire Home in Dublin city centre with his friend Ursula Hegarty, who'd also grown up in the hospital.

'We're doing our best to change the place from the inside, Martin, like you did in Baldoyle Hospital,' Hubert said, 'but they make us feel like upstarts just for asking the staff to knock on our bedroom doors before they come in.'

We had started meeting regularly around that long table to discuss areas in which we could target change. We spoke a lot about what the American Independent Living movement called 'The Pillars of Independent Living': housing, equipment, personal assistance, transport, access and peer support. All these elements had to be tackled for meaningful Independent Living to be achieved. What was the point in having a wheelchair-accessible house if the person living in it didn't have the assistance to get out of bed in the morning, or the transport to get to work?

But we had to start somewhere, and some of us were getting impatient. In the summer of 1991, while I was gathering the paperwork for my Morrison application, a group of us broke away to found an organisation that would campaign for funding for assistance services along the lines of those on offer in the US.

Our smaller group started meeting several times a week in The Royal Dublin Hotel on O'Connell Street, one of the few places in the city with level access and a usable toilet, and by March 1992 we had formally named ourselves 'The Dublin Center for Independent Living'.

The founding members were Hubert and Ursula, plus four other wheelchair users, Michael McCabe, Dermot Walsh, Declan O'Keeffe and Peter Moore, and one non-disabled person, a law student called Catherine Hickey. I was a founder, but I left my name off all the documents because I wanted to be seen to act or speak independently when this suited our political objectives.

We spelled 'Center' the American way as a nod of gratitude to the people who had inspired us, but the US term 'Personal Care Attendants' didn't sit well with us. It made us think of being 'cared for', which was what we were trying to get away from. Instead, we decided we would campaign for funding for 'Personal Assistants' or 'PAs', and any time we had an opportunity, we explained the word 'personal' was there because their tasks would be 'personally' directed by the disabled people they worked for, who we called the 'leaders'. This time we were going to be giving instructions, not following them.

Subtleties of language may seem small matters, but I knew the way we talked would shape how other people thought, and how we thought ourselves. We had constantly to remind ourselves what we were about. We didn't want to become a hierarchical organisation that provided services to a rigid formula; we saw ourselves as a collective of individuals who were looking for freedom and had come together to create the supports we, and others like us, needed.

We were soon given a small room in the gate lodge of the Carmichael Centre for Voluntary Groups on North Brunswick Street, and as we started drawing up plans, we spoke regularly with our American counterparts and with Independent Living groups in European countries. Jana Overbo, an outspoken young disabled activist from Berkeley, California, came over to become our information officer. Jana had been living independently with PA support for years, and she knew hundreds of other disabled people who did the same; this was ordinary stuff to her. It was down to me and Jana to help the other founders visualise how this was going to work, and to dispel any worries they had.

We went straight to work, applying for European funding for a pilot project in which we proposed to train twenty-five assistants to support fifteen significantly disabled people to leave institutions or family homes and move into independent accommodation. The first fifteen candidates would include Hubert and the other founders – and me, if I was still in Dublin when the money came in.

I was the only participant already living independently, but with my J1 income down, I was feeling the strain of paying for nearly twenty-four-hour support. At this stage, there was hardly a lad in Baldoyle who hadn't done a stint with me, and I had become a hand-me-down from older brother to younger brother. Big Bren's teenage daughter Sandra had even started earning pocket money cooking me meals, and one of her pals, Eoin Healy, who lived a few houses away, had become my latest recruit for night shifts. (I could only pay around twenty quid a night, but I was still throwing in driving lessons, and Eoin also did his best to help me give up smoking by getting through more than half a packet of my cigarettes each night.)

Never Know Your Place

While we waited on news of our funding application (and I waited on news of my visa), we were helped in our efforts to raise public awareness by a new friend of mine, a charismatic young journalist from Mayo called Donal Toolan. Donal was a wheelchair user himself, and his RTÉ television programmes 'Not so Different' and 'In From the Margins' brought issues such as the institutionalisation of disabled adults into Irish family living rooms for the first time.

In June 1992, I gave an interview to *The Irish Times* in which I tried to describe what it was like to live in a residential institution, with no control

Martin takes his opportunity to get the ear of President Mary Robinson at an event in the early 1990s. Martin and other key activists such as journalist Donal Toolan were working hard in this period to raise awareness of disability issues, and President Robinson was known to have an interest in disability rights and legislation.

Throwing out the Rule Book

over things like when you went to bed or what food you ate.

'All the daily needs are reasonably well catered for, but only within the four walls of the residential centre,' I said.

I didn't want to depict the institutions simplistically. They weren't all terrible places, and many were trying to improve, but I wanted the public to think about how it felt to be confined in that way. It didn't matter how 'severely disabled' a person's body was, their mind, brain and spirit craved independence. The only solution was to give disabled people their freedom by letting them move into homes of their own and funding PAs to support them with the tasks of everyday living and working.

I wanted to let them know there was nothing far-fetched about the idea. 'It started off in California twenty-five years ago with the whole notion of "let's empower the individual",' I told the journalist. '"Let's give the individual the resources instead of handing over large sums of money to institutions."'

Providing assistance in private homes could cost the State less, I argued. All we were asking for was a chance to run a pilot for two years.

Just as I sensed people in Ireland were starting to sit up and take note of what we were proposing, I got news that my Morrison visa had been approved. The visa was based on a loose job offer I'd received from the Center for Independent Living in Berkeley and I had four months in which to make my travel plans and finish up my business this side of the Atlantic.

I was on a high for weeks after the visa approval came in, knowing for certain that America hadn't seen my disability as a barrier. But then my body threw a spanner in the works. A bus load of us had gone on a trip to the UK to meet other Independent Living groups, and on the last day, I had a fall getting out of bed in the hotel in Holyhead. It was the sort of fall

Never Know Your Place

An exhausted Martin Naughton asleep on a road trip. He undertook various gruelling trips to the UK and Denmark to meet and learn from other Independent Living groups. The young man behind him is his nephew Eoin McConville (son of his sister Cait) who accompanied him on occasions along with PAs like Robby Martin.

I'd always feared. The doctor in the local hospital said I had so many breaks and sprains it wasn't worth counting. He just covered me with emergency supports and put me on a stretcher to get me through the ferry journey home.

By the time I arrived at the Emergency Department in Beaumont in Dublin, I was struggling to keep my spirits up. The surgeon, Ray Moran, examined me and said my bones were too brittle to operate on.

'The less interference the better,' he said. 'There's no rule book for your body. This is something yourself and myself are going to have to manage

Throwing out the Rule Book

using our intuition. Just come in to me every week and I'll check you over.'

This wasn't a conventional approach but at least he was acknowledging there was nothing normal about my body. I may have been in a sorry state, but having a doctor treat me as a thinking adult made me feel ten feet tall.

I had long suspected that doctors were winging it when it came to my condition – and a few years earlier they had even changed my diagnosis from muscular dystrophy to spinal muscular atrophy. Here was a doctor with the decency to admit it.

I began to wonder, was it time to start listening to my own body and taking responsibility for the management of my own health? 'Forget doctor knows best', as the guys in Boston said. It was an empowering concept but not easy for someone who had grown up listening to the emotionless voices of medics, endlessly reminding me of my physical vulnerability.

As it turned out, by November I was right as rain. My only problem was that the four-month window of my Morrison visa had expired and I had to re-apply. I couldn't help thinking to myself, surely the Americans will turn me down now they've gotten a second chance. But I was wrong.

Chapter 19

Know your Story

In January 1993, I said what I expected to be my final goodbye to my father, and I boarded my flight to Boston. I arrived with an entourage of three assistants: my old regular Robby Martin; Dermot Healy, a twenty-something Galway guy with a forehead like Elvis, who'd been with me on that trip to the UK and through my recovery; and a recent recruit, seventeen-year-old Bob Waldron, who was the son of another of my Baldoyle neighbours.

All three lads were waiting on their own Morrison visa applications, but they'd promised at least one of them would stay with me for a few months until I was settled. After my fall, I wasn't going to take any risks. Although I'd no intention of returning to Ireland, I'd purchased an open-ended, two-way ticket to ensure my traveller's medical insurance was valid. The plan was to spend two weeks with my sister Chris in Boston, catching up with family and friends before setting out on a road trip to California to begin my job in Berkeley.

Over the years, Chris's husband, Noel, had improvised various ramps to help me access the main floor of their house, but with their sons now away at college, it seemed unfair to expect Noel and whichever of my PAs was on duty to haul me up, so I asked my friends in Boston Center for Independent

Know your Story

The home of Martin's sister Chris and her family with snow on the ground, taken by Martin's first PA, Robby Martin, when they arrived – hoping to stay in the US for good – in January 1993.

Living for advice. They suggested I drive out to Concord, twenty miles west of Boston, to meet one of their founders, a man called Fred Fay. I was told Fred could lend me a special kind of ramp. And besides, they said, Fred was someone I had to meet. He might even have some work for me.

I'd heard a little about Fred and I knew he was one of the activists credited with winning support for the Americans with Disabilities Act of 1990, a major piece of civil rights legislation that prohibited discrimination.

Robby, Dermot and Bob all decided to come along on the drive to Concord in the rusty Ford Crown Victoria I'd bought earlier in the week. I'd told them they could head off for a few hours of sightseeing after they got me settled in. This was likely to be a long meeting.

Never Know Your Place

We drove up the wooded driveway to Fred's clapboard bungalow. Fred's partner, Trish Irons, answered the door. 'Welcome to Concord, guys from Ireland,' she said, with a smile, and led us through an open-plan living area into a big bedroom with a cathedral ceiling. Fred, a bearded middle-aged guy, was lying stretched out in a metal bed, with wires, remote controls and mirrors dangling from a frame above his head. My heart sank. This was pretty depressing, like visiting someone in a hospital.

As Robby, Dermot and Bob turned to leave, I muttered under my breath, 'Change of plan. Don't go far. I'll be out of here in half an hour.'

This Fred Fay wasn't going to be any help to me. How could there be any vibrancy in a man who looked as if he was on his deathbed?

While the lads watched HBO in the living room next door, Fred started talking – all the time looking me straight in the eye via a round shaving mirror suspended above his forehead. There was a mirror on the ceiling too and I began to realise that these mirrors were part of a carefully constructed system that allowed him to see 360 degrees while lying on his back. Not only could he see me beside him, but he could also see who was coming up the drive. Monitors and keyboards were lined up on metal shelves near his bed, and he used the remote controls that dangled from the frame above him to do tasks like answer calls and move his bed.

Seeing my interest, Fred said he'd worked for IBM when he was younger, and it was thanks to technology he was now able to work from his bed. He told me how he'd drummed up support for campaigns by calling hundreds of organisations, linking up people who would never otherwise have crossed paths. Nowadays, he said much of his time was spent liaising with Government officials on disability matters and writing political speeches.

His voice was gravelly and his mouth barely opened as he talked, but his eyes danced around and there was something light-hearted and boyish about him.

'If it wasn't for technology,' he said, 'I'd be bored out of my mind.'

Our conversation was interrupted by a phone call from somebody on President Clinton's staff. Clinton was in his first month in office and as I listened, it became clear Fred was a trusted member of a panel that was preparing to interview high-profile disability activist Judy Heumann for a job in Clinton's administration.

I was astonished by the political reach and charisma of this immobile man. Though he must have told the story a thousand times, he satisfied my curiosity by telling me how he'd been paralysed at the age of sixteen doing gymnastics in his backyard, and had spent many years as a wheelchair user before being diagnosed with an inoperable spinal cyst. If he sat up, the cyst inhibited his breathing.

'Pretty quickly it would be lights out,' he said.

Fred hadn't left his bed for thirty years. 'I want more time and staying horizontal is the price I have to pay.'

It seemed a horrendous level of restriction, but he'd done a lot of things in this state, including meeting his partner Trish.

Fred asked about the situation for disabled people in Ireland.

'And who is going to sort it all out now you're over here?' he asked without pausing for an answer.

I could see Fred had an ability to connect with all sorts of people, on the telephone or in person, and put them at ease. Here was a man who had plenty to teach me. I was starting to feel pleasantly relaxed in his company.

As it grew dark, Dermot Healy stuck his head in to see how we were

Never Know Your Place

getting on and soon he and Fred were deep in conversation about *Star Trek*. I could hardly get a word in.

We ended up staying the night and the next day, Fred offered me a few weeks' work, plus the loan of the decent ramp I'd come for. He said he needed to find out if the Americans with Disabilities Act he'd fought so hard for was working. I was to act as his envoy, meeting activists across the US, and reporting back.

'What is the level of awareness of the Act? I want to know, Martin. What are the major stumbling blocks around its implementation?'

A long list of stop-offs was drawn up on a fold-out map, starting with St Louis, circling back towards Philadelphia, down to Washington DC, and back to Concord to update Fred, before heading west to California.

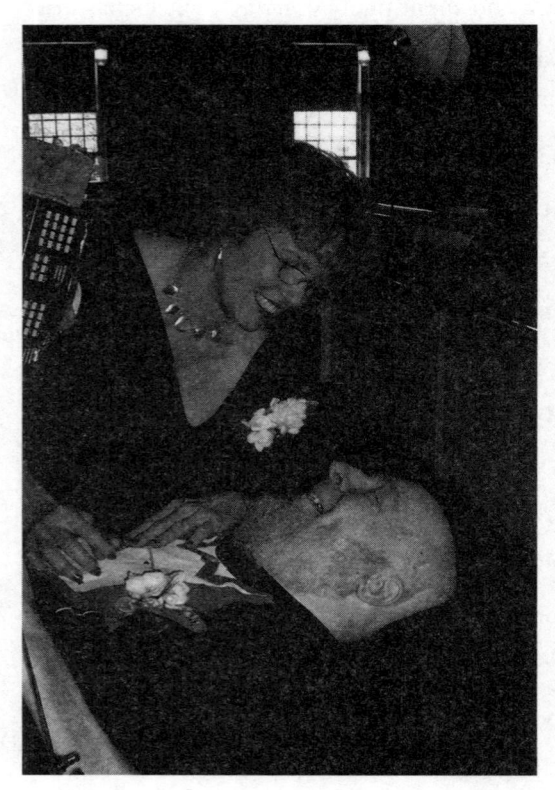

American activist Fred Fay with his partner Trish Irons, photographed at the wedding of Trish's daughter. Fred and Trish lived together from 1983 until Fred's death in 2011. Fred and Trish made private vows but were not legally married, though Trish often referred to Fred as her husband so people would know she was not his Personal Assistant.

Know your Story

Part of my appeal was that I had purchased a video camera a couple of years before and was known for carrying it everywhere I went. I would direct whoever was assisting me to film anything that might be worth sharing, such as an example of good access to a building.

I had my camera with me that day at Fred's house, and he immediately realised its usefulness. I could be his eyes on the road.

A few days later, we hit the road in the Crown Victoria and began to work through Fred's itinerary. There were dozens of disability groups, but wherever I went, a call from Fred opened doors and ensured we were treated like kings.

While I was his ambassador, Fred said it was good for me to learn more about the history of disability and the civil rights movement. He'd link into every meeting by phone and before he put the phone down at the end, he'd say, 'Before Martin leaves you, will you make sure he knows your story?'

He said he wanted me to understand that every regional group of disabled people had its own history and culture, and in each case a local leader had emerged to lead change for their people.

I started to wonder if Fred was sending me a message that my responsibility lay back in Ireland. But if he was, I wasn't ready to hear it. Driving around the States in my Crown Victoria was too much fun. Unfortunately, Robby, whose responsibility it had been to maintain the car, had returned home when his visa was rejected on account of his past misdemeanours. His replacement was Virginia, a no-nonsense thirty-something from New Zealand, who had convinced me to give her the job based on her knowledge of vehicle maintenance.

'There isn't much I can't do myself,' she had told me in the interview.

Then, sensing my initial hesitation at hiring a woman, she had added,

Never Know Your Place

with justifiable reproach, 'Don't worry, I also know how to flutter my eyelashes at a mechanic.'

Dermot, Bob and Virginia took turns at the wheel. The rule was that every time the tank emptied, the next shift would start. Virginia's shifts were the shortest because she drove so fast. The main topic of conversation was the weather, and whether the Crown Victoria could hold up to it. In Philadelphia, we tested it by breaking our way out of our motel after a heavy snowstorm. It was the day of Bob's eighteenth birthday and off we chugged, scraping the underbody of the car along the compacted snow. But we made it to the Interstate, and as we drove along, one of those overhead electric signs flashed above, saying 'Happy Birthday, Bob'. It must have been another Bob, but it felt like a message from the heavens urging us on.

When we got to Washington DC, my first meeting was with Judy Heumann, who, after that phone call at Fred's house, had been appointed to Clinton's administration as Assistant Secretary for the Office of Special Education.

Judy and I hit it off straightaway as we chatted in her office in the US Government buildings. She was a vocal but level-headed New Yorker from a Jewish family. Growing up, she had narrowly avoided institutionalisation, and she told me how she'd spent much of her childhood fighting for access to education after being turned down from local schools for being a fire hazard. She laughed hard when I told her about some of my exploits in Baldoyle Hospital.

Even though she wasn't much more than forty, it was Judy who had led the disability rights 'sit-ins' on Madison Avenue and in San Francisco two decades earlier and had helped bring about seminal legislation such as Section 504 of the Americans with Disabilities Act of 1973, and key

Know your Story

Judy Heumann, who Martin got to know through Fred Fay, at the legendary 504 protests in the 1970s. Judy died in 2023.

amendments to the Act.[8]

'You know people just love to say "no" when you ask for something, Martin,' she said. 'You gotta make so much noise that's it's easier for them to say "yes".'

I could see Judy knew how to get things done – when to work within the system and when to fight it. 'Here's a person I can come back to if I ever need political clear-thinking,' I thought.

My final meeting was with Justin Dart, Jr, a veteran activist who had been a signatory to the Americans with Disabilities Act. Dart was older and wore cowboy boots and a Stetson hat with a pin of the American flag

Never Know Your Place

on the band. He was impatient when I arrived in his large office, and I could see he was thinking, 'Who is this funny-looking guy in a tweed cap and why has Fred asked me to see him?' But he softened when I started talking and I ended up spending the evening listening to political anecdotes at a downtown restaurant with him and his friends.

I'd promised Fred I'd brief him the next day, so Bob and Virginia collected me from the restaurant at midnight, and we began the drive to Concord. All three of us were smoking hard as Virginia drove us through the Fort McHenry Tunnel in Maryland, and as we exited, the cops pulled up alongside, signalling for us to pull in.

'You're smoking,' the officer said as Virginia wound down the window.

'Ah no,' I thought. Bob may have turned eighteen, but he looked young and the legal age for smoking was twenty-one.

'Your tail pipe is smoking,' the officer added.

'Ah, we know that,' we all thought with relief. The Crown Victoria had been smoking since St Louis.

It was April by the time I made it to California. It had been an eye-opening few months on the road, and I'd seen how powerful disability was in American politics.

Fred claimed the disability vote had given Republican vice-president George HW Bush his landslide win over Democratic nominee Michael Dukakis in 1988, and when four years later Fred had switched sides, he and Judy had helped bring Clinton to power.

At the Center for Independent Living in Berkeley I tried to suss out more about the vague job I'd been promised, but it was hard to get straight answers.

I'd arrived in the middle of a campaign to fight welfare cutbacks being

Know your Story

implemented by Republican Governor Pete Wilson. I tried to make myself useful, making video interviews of activists, sending copies to Dublin and to Fred. I paid attention to how my colleagues were living: their homes, their adapted vans, the way they managed their Personal Assistants.

The place was still being run by one of its founders, Ed Roberts, who used a motorised wheelchair and slept in an 'iron lung' machine to stimulate his breathing. 'This is a global struggle for freedom, and we got to help each other,' he told me at his house one night. He said he had people working in Russia and the Eastern Bloc, and the next day a big group of activists returned from a long stay in Japan (I couldn't help but notice some of them had brought Japanese girlfriends with them).

All this talk about spreading the word was making me think. A few years earlier, I'd looked on America as a place where I could build a future for myself, a future based on money and quality of life. But somehow I'd been drawn back into the world of disability. I was making daily phone calls to the Center for Independent Living in Dublin. The funding for the pilot programme had finally come through, but they sounded like they were losing confidence.

At the back of my mind, I could hear Fred asking, 'What's *your* story?' In my heart I knew the answer. I was just an Irish lad with a disability, reared behind the walls of an institution, who'd won his freedom thanks to a strong will and the gift of the gab. I'd escaped the hospital – and now Ireland. But what about the other people I'd left behind; all the people still living in institutions? If I didn't go back for them, who would?

With duty on my mind, I called my sister Chris.

'Dad's been in the hospital for weeks,' she said. 'But Maureen says he won't let go. We think he's waiting for you to come home before he'll die.'

Never Know Your Place

I looked at the open ticket I still carried in my wallet and knew what I had to do.

When I arrived at University Hospital Galway, I pulled out a little bottle of whiskey that I'd got on the plane, and Dad and I shared it. He was pleased to see me, but too weak to make a big deal about it, or to watch the video interviews I'd made of his brother and old friends in Boston. I was upset to see how he'd lost the will to live, but when I arrived back in Dublin, the doctor rang and said there'd been an improvement. There was a smile back on Dad's face, and he was inquisitive and eating.

But it must have been the hunger of dying, *'ocras an bháis'*, as they always used to say in Spiddal, because the next day he was gone.

Chapter 20

Operation Get-Out

I thought a lot about Fred Fay in the months after I returned to Ireland. How he lived by his instincts, knowing who to talk to and when, making himself useful, taking every opportunity. How he gathered fragments of information, making sure he was the only one who had the whole picture. And all with the aim of clearing a path so he could achieve what he wanted. I could see how Fred did it because it wasn't so different from the way I lived my own life.

Once I let it be known I was back in Ireland to stay, it was accepted I would resume leadership of the Center for Independent Living in Dublin. The founder members had been joined by new recruits, and everyone was full of energy but overwhelmed about how to run the PA programme.

You have to remember that many of the people involved were not only organising the programme, but they were also part of it.

'Don't go getting too comfortable in your homes,' I told them as we crammed into our weekly meeting in our gate lodge office.

'We are leading this, and we need to make damn sure we are seen everywhere in Dublin with our PAs in tow. Visibility is key.'

I knew it was only by seeing us that the public would get their heads around the concept.

Never Know Your Place

A strategy meeting of CIL activists at Carmichael Lodge, probably in 1995. To Martin's left is fellow CIL founder Peter Moore and sitting on the floor is Gráinne McGettrick, CIL's research officer.

From the start, we all knew it was more than a pilot. Our intention was to secure long-term Government funding for PA services. The European funding had given us £500,000. That was going to cover twenty-five personal assistants for fifteen people for a year or two at most. With thousands of disabled people in institutions all over Ireland, it was a drop in the ocean. We had to keep focused on the bigger picture.

Having given up my American dream for this, I was single-minded. I had no shame in asking anyone for money because I believed wholeheartedly that disabled people had the right to live independently. 'If you don't ask, you don't get,' and I was the man to do the asking. Failing would have

Operation Get-Out

been a personal failure, but I knew it was going to be the mother and father of all battles.

Conveniently, the Minister for Social Welfare and Family Affairs in the Fianna Fáil–Labour Party coalition was Michael Woods, my local TD from Baldoyle, the man who had promised his door would always be open. The first thing I did was to go to his department and say, 'You know we can create jobs through our PA programme,' and they handed us £50,000 a year. Then I went to FÁS and said, 'We want these jobs to be sustainable over a long period,' and we came away with an agreement that every PA would be taken on under the FÁS training scheme, providing us with seventy percent of each salary. Our half a million was growing.

Once the first fifteen of our people had left institutions or family homes and begun to adjust to living with PA support, we started training PAs for a second, more ambitious project, which we called 'Operation Get-Out'. This was a similar programme but aimed at people with an even higher level of support need. We went round the Cheshire Homes in Dublin and pinned 'Operation Get-Out' posters on noticeboards. The staff didn't try to stop us – they knew they couldn't suppress what we were doing. The people we were targeting were the ones who didn't see newspapers, who couldn't get to our meetings, who were cut off from the world. We wanted to give these people an opportunity to be free at last.

Many of those who responded were very afraid.

'What if it doesn't work out and we've lost our place?' they asked when we called out to meet them. 'We could end up somewhere worse.'

So we spoke to the management of the Cheshire Homes, and to their credit, they agreed to guarantee each person's place for one year. They understood the security would take a weight off people's shoulders. You

Never Know Your Place

have to remember almost no one had done this before. It's not easy being the first to jump.

One of the quickest people to sign up was a woman in her mid-thirties called Mairéad Manton. Mairéad had been a few years behind me in Baldoyle Hospital and had lived in three different Cheshire Homes since. She had cerebral palsy and communicated using a primitive 'lightwriter' keyboard that displayed typed words on a small screen.[9]

'Why do you want to leave this place?' we asked her.

She typed her answer: 'C-O-M-F-O-R-T-A-B-L-E P-R-I-S-O-N.'

Mairéad left the Cheshire Home and moved into a rented flat in Sandymount. At first, everything that could go wrong, went wrong. Frequent miscommunication with her PAs meant that sometimes two would show up, sometimes none. She found it hard to explain the ground rules to her PAs, like not helping themselves to her food. She got locked out and locked in. The money she'd made from selling the *Big Issue* was swiped. She even got hit by a car. But never for a moment did she question her decision. She raced along the streets between Sandymount and the city centre like her wheelchair was a Formula One car, drank wine with friends, wrote poems for the people she cared about.

'T-I-R-E-D B-U-T H-A-P-P-Y' she typed one evening as we talked in the bar at the Royal Dublin Hotel.

'A B-E-G-I-N-N-I-N-G' she added.

'I'd take my hat off to you any day, Mairéad,' I told her. 'You were brave enough to step out into a world that was utterly unknown.'

I meant it. Hers was the greatest kind of success story. It left its mark on my heart.

But not every participant flourished. Two brothers were finding

Operation Get-Out

Mairéad Manton, one of the first people to sign up for Operation Get-Out, and a person for whom Martin had particular admiration. Having lived up until her thirties in various institutions, starting with Baldoyle Hospital, she adapted to Independent Living with the support of PAs and lived in her own home until her death in 2018.

Independent Living particularly hard. One of our newer staff, a Serbian disabled activist called Gordana Rajkov, visited the brothers' apartment and found it lacking in basic items such as plates, cutlery and sheets. She suggested they go shopping together, and in the bedding section of Roches Stores, she asked, 'Well, what bedding do you like?'

One of the brothers answered, 'Which one do you like?'

Gordana persevered. 'It's not about the one I like. Which one do you like?'

If you haven't experienced institutionalisation, it is impossible to imagine how difficult these small decisions can be for a person who has lived in an

Never Know Your Place

institution for decades, with no input into the dynamics of ordinary life.

In the end, one of those brothers went back to a Cheshire Home, having decided Independent Living wasn't for him. I remember being disappointed at first, but then I insisted we celebrate anyway.

'At least he's had an opportunity to make his choice,' I told my fellow activists. 'Nobody before him had that.'

By spring 1994, we had three small offices up and running: the gate lodge at Carmichael House for operations; a room in the Union building on Parnell Square for our communications people; and a shop front on Bolton Street for the money side. This scattered set-up suited me. I moved between all three offices, acting as the conduit and information-gatherer. It also had the effect of creating energy when people came together for a meeting in our 'head office', which everyone knew was the Royal Dublin Hotel: the only place in Dublin that could accommodate twenty plus wheelchair users and their PAs, and make us feel very welcome too.

My office was the dark blue Renault Traffic I'd invested in on my return from America. Eoin Healy, the young lad who had done night shifts before I went to America, was now one of my fulltime PAs. I'd instruct him to park the van in a wheelchair spot next to the school on North Brunswick Street or in front of our shop on Bolton Street, and the van could be sitting there for hours, while I held meetings and took calls on my car phone. The van had tinted windows and everyone said it looked like the FBI were doing a stake-out – although if I had John Farnham's 'You're the Voice' blasting out of the cassette player, as I often did, that spoiled the image.

Word got around about what we were doing. Our conviction that this was nothing less than a civil rights battle of global importance meant that educated and creative non-disabled people gravitated towards us, people

Operation Get-Out

like playwright Christian O'Reilly, who worked with one of our founder members Dermot Walsh in our Parnell Square communications office.[10] These people were also drawn by the part-time jobs we had on offer, but one of our unwritten rules was that everyone had to do a stint as a PA. If they didn't do this, how could they understand what the service meant to individuals?

Our offices took on a social vibe, and politicised musicians like Christy Moore, Christy Dignam and Liam Ó Maonlaí, people who had a genuine curiosity about disability and an instinctive sense of the injustice of our forced separation from Irish society, started to come to events or teach song-writing workshops organised by Hubert McCormack. There was a buzz about everything we did. At one meeting in Carmichael House, I asked a hairy-looking fellow with glasses who was standing by the kitchen door to make the tea.

Hubert pulled me aside afterwards.

'That fellow you got to make the tea,' he said.

'Yes,' I said.

'That was Bono, you know.'

'Oh. Well, in fairness, he made it.'

Those funny moments, and the inevitable crushes and gossip as people mixed and enjoyed their new freedom – like college students coming of age – provided relief from what could at times be oppressively serious work.

By June 1994, we had only six months left of our European funding, and we were overspending each week. But with people's lives transforming before our eyes, how could we ration services or watch pennies? We were also getting calls from disabled people in other parts of Ireland – people in Waterford, in Clare, in Donegal – who'd heard what we were doing and wanted to get out of institutions themselves, or help friends get out. We

Never Know Your Place

wanted to be in a position to support them.

I kept thinking about strategy. With many other organisations likely to be in the same boat at the end of the funding period, how could we get ourselves to the front of the queue?

I rang Judy Heumann in DC and within minutes I had the answer. We wouldn't wait six months; we'd bring the crisis forward, tell the Government we'd already run out of money. That way we'd have the stage to ourselves.

On 28 June, the morning of the last session of the Dáil before the summer break in 1994, we placed our PAs on protective notice and about forty of us gathered at the Dáil gates with placards saying things like, 'Choice Not Charity'.

When politicians stopped to ask what it was about, we told them: 'Give us proper funding or you will be sending us back to institutions.'

I tried to appear bullish, but I was worried. We'd organised small protests about inaccessible public transport at bus stops and train stations before, but nothing of this scale.

Many of the activists had grown up with me in Baldoyle Hospital – people such as Mairéad Manton, Hubert McCormack, Ursula Hegarty and Rosaleen McDonagh. Our friendship and shared experience was our strength, but with no wheelchair-accessible toilets nearby and many people who, like me, struggled to regulate their body temperature, the physical discomfort was significant.[11]

We had brought duvets and blankets, flasks of hot drinks and boxes of sandwiches, and a couple of bottles of brandy that we passed under our cloaks, but when there was no response from the Government by the evening, my spirits fell.

'They won't break us, Martin,' Hubert said, and with his powerful voice,

Operation Get-Out

Above: Martin and fellow activists protest outside the Dáil in June 1994.

Below left & right: While securing funding for PA services was the top priority for Martin and his fellow CIL activists, in 1995 they also protested to highlight inaccessible public transport, which was another barrier to Independent Living.

Never Know Your Place

he lifted us all with a rendition of Christy Moore's 'The Voyage', a song that had become an anthem for our journey to independence.

As the song finished, Mary Llewellyn, who knew about the sit-in and must have been worried, arrived from Donnycarney on her bike with a rucksack containing three hot water bottles.

'This is about equality,' I whispered to her. 'I don't think it looks good to be the only one with a personal supply of hot-water bottles.'

'You're no good to anyone if you freeze to bloody death,' she said. She wouldn't leave until I let her stuff the hot-water bottles down the back and sides of my chair.

At 6am, the mother of one of the other activists, James Brosnan, arrived (bless her) with a van-load of breakfast rolls. Rashers, sausages, pudding – the works. This time, there was one for everyone in the audience, and even the Guards outside Dáil Éireann couldn't resist.

On the second day, junior Government officials started coming out, trying to placate us with assurances, but we didn't budge because when it came to politics, one of the rules I lived by was, 'If it's not in writing, it never happened'.

At about 4am on the second night, Minister for Health Brendan Howlin came out to us with a copy of a statement he had just released. The statement said our PA programmes would be funded for a further three to six months while the Government conducted an evaluation. Alright, I said. We can work with this. They have unlocked the cash box.

But our victory was short-lived because, on 17 November, just as we were about to launch a five-year plan for a national PA service, we got news that the Government was about to be toppled.

What followed was the most difficult year of my life. Everything we'd

Above: Liam Ó Maonlaí was one of a number of musicians and artists who expressed solidarity with disabled activists. He is pictured with Martin and CIL activist Jana Overbo in May 1995 at the international symposium 'Disability – Investment not Burden' in Jury's Hotel.
Below: Liam Ó Maonlaí, Martin and Jana Overbo in Jury's Hotel in May 1995. Martin's old friend Dermot Mooney can be seen to his left – still supporting Martin over three decades after they first met in Baldoyle Hospital.

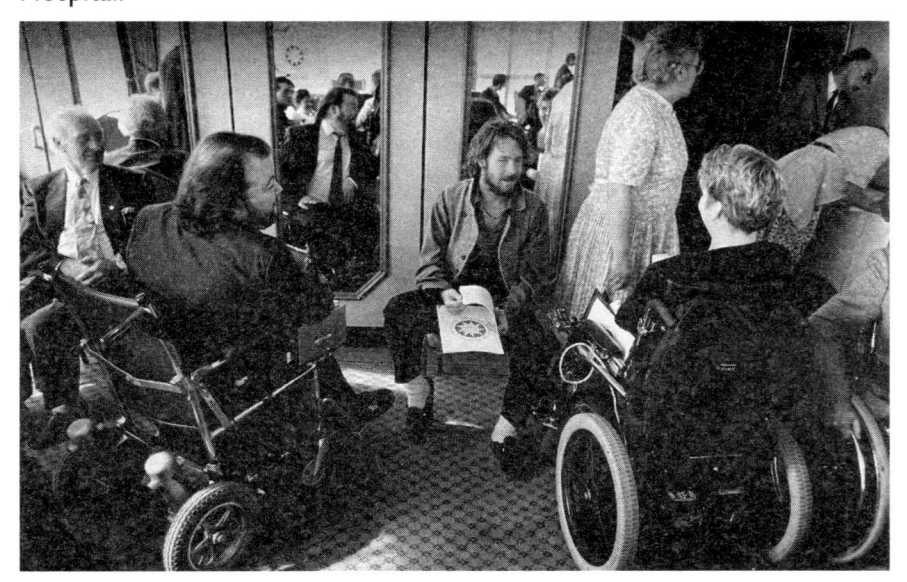

Never Know Your Place

worked towards seemed bathed in uncertainty. With a new Government and a new Minister for Health, Michael Noonan, I was in unknown political territory. All we could do was make as much 'noise' as possible, to make sure the new Government knew we weren't going away. We issued a stream of reports and press releases, and organised impromptu sit-ins nearly every week at public buildings or transport hubs – 'dropping bombs on the establishment,' I liked to call it. [12]

In May 1995, with still no news on the evaluation, we organised an international symposium called 'Disability – Investment not Burden' in Jury's Hotel. Liam Ó Maonlaí chaired the event, and human rights lawyer Gerard Quinn gave a speech, in which he set out what it would cost the Government to give disabled people a chance of living daily life the way other people did. 'This investment makes sense!' he told the audience. [13]

Afterwards, I was smoking in the Coffee Dock in Jury's when I saw Minister Noonan walk by. I knew I had to take my opportunity and I caught up with him in the toilets.

'I know what you are going to ask me,' he said as he walked towards the door. 'I want to tell you that you have nothing to worry about. It's put to bed.'

In September 1995, Martin received a 'Person of the Year' Award, which he used as another platform to say publicly to Government, 'Now, don't forget what you promised us!'

Operation Get-Out

That night was the first night I'd slept well in years.

* * *

In June 1995, the Government evaluation report supporting the PA service was at last published, and by September we began formal negotiations with the Department of Health in Hawkins House. The officials were aggressive negotiators, hell-bent on keeping costs low. It was a pressurised situation, and I came down with Bell's palsy, but I dragged myself up every morning because I had to be there to push back.

Fortunately, the negotiators had a few blind spots. Of particular use were the copies of the files relating to the negotiations I was being given each night by an informer in the Department of Health.

In November 1995, I was in our gate lodge office on North Brunswick Street when a courier arrived with an envelope addressed to me. Inside was a copy of a Government announcement confirming a deal had been signed off: Personal Assistance was to become a State-funded service that any disabled person in Ireland could apply for.

We had at last secured Irish State money that would give thousands of disabled people in institutions the prospect of a way out.

After I'd shared it with everyone in the office, one of the first things I did was ring Barbara. It was rare for us to talk about anything other than family stuff, but this felt like personal news.

'Great achievement, Martin,' she said. 'You took on the wall that divides us from the outside world.' And in her characteristic no-nonsense way, she ended the subject by saying, 'But you were only asking for what is right.'

I remember putting the phone down and feeling the shivery tiredness that accompanies relief come over me. The door to the yard outside was open and I could see Eoin Healy sitting on the wall smoking and

Never Know Your Place

talking to some other PAs.

'Time to go home, Eoin,' I called, making my way towards the door.

We crossed the street to where the van was parked and Eoin pushed me up the ramp into the back, straightened my hat, lit a cigarette for me and one for himself, and we headed off towards Dorset Street and northwards out of the city.

'Blast up the heat, Eoin, will you? And take that phone off the hook for a bit,' I called. 'And put your foot on it.'

The smoke began to fill the van, and as I leant back in my chair and looked out the window – past Croke Park, over Annesley Bridge and into Fairview – I went over the twists and turns of the year in my head.

I thought about the political instincts that had sustained me through that torturous campaign, how they were the product of my institutional childhood. I had learnt to read situations quickly in Baldoyle Hospital. Who was an ally? Who was a threat? Where did the power lie? It was there I had learnt the subtle art of rebelling and asking for more without alienating the authorities.

Nobody is born political, I thought. Circumstances make you that way. I wouldn't have wished my childhood on anyone, but I felt satisfaction that afternoon, knowing I'd used those hard-earned instincts to change the life of disabled people in Ireland forever.

I still had many battles ahead. We all did. But this was a beginning. We'd set fire to the rocks, broken the ground and put down foundations that we could build on.

Epilogue

A lot has happened in my life and in politics in the twenty years since we won that landmark PA funding campaign. But that's another story. I know I wouldn't have made it to sixty-two years of age without my PAs. I mean that literally. From the day I left Baldoyle Hospital, my PAs (unofficial and official) have been with me twenty-four hours a day, turning me as I sleep, helping me in and out of bed and to the bathroom, preparing meals with me, driving me to meetings and enabling me to work and pay taxes.

All human beings are dependent on others, but having a disability intensifies that dependency. Without adequate support, a disabled person like me could easily become vulnerable.

In the twenty years since funded PA services were introduced, hundreds of others have left institutions as I did, or avoided going into them in the first place. Instead of living in an impersonal public space and following a daily routine set by staff, they live in their own homes and move through each day according to their private rhythms.

Like many who once lived by institutional rules, I have a deep appreciation of the sweetness of personal freedom. It's a joy to get up in the morning at a time of my choosing; to have a bacon sandwich and a mug of tea (I finally gave up the Carrolls for good, in case you are wondering); to juggle phone calls and impromptu visits from neighbours; to eat my meals when I feel hungry; to sit at the little desk in my front room and listen back to these words as they play on my text-to-voice software.

My home these days is a single-storey cottage on the busy main street

Never Know Your Place

that runs through Baldoyle Village. I moved here not long after that PA campaign. It's newer than the cottages around it, purpose-built to be wheelchair accessible, with two small bedrooms: one for me and one for whichever of my PAs is on duty.

When you have PAs in your life, it's hard to be lonely. Your home is a hive of activity. Many of my PAs, including my current team, Mladen (from Bosnia), Marco (from Italy), and Sang, Hung and Quong (from Vietnam), have made me feel like an honorary family member. I've loved hearing about their cultures, learning to say goodnight in different languages, getting to know their partners and children. Keeping the company of younger people has kept me young in spirit, while others of my generation have grown old. I wonder sometimes what it would have been like to have had my own children.

I left Baldoyle Hospital behind, but I never left the community that became my second home. Through my living-room window I see a procession of familiar faces walking or wheeling past, many waving in at me. Across the road is the row of painted cottages where Al Neehan once had his shoe repair shop, and a little further up, the bus stop where Barbara, Mairéad, Micheál Ó Bríain and I got off the bus that October afternoon in 1963. Behind the lifeless convent building that fronts the street looms the grey north wing of Baldoyle Hospital. It's still in operation, but the Sisters of Charity have left and it is under new management. I haven't been inside in decades.

Kit Byrne's old house is across the road and around the corner. He died in 2014 and without him the village of Baldoyle isn't the same. Telling this story, I have found myself thinking of Kit Byrne, and of Dermot Mooney, again and again.

Epilogue

Kit, with his simple human decency, did more for the hospital children than any senior staff member. He was the person who encouraged us to reach for the skies, and the first to catch us if we didn't make it.

Born without privilege, Kit had no choice but to work within the system. In a world where respect for religious orders was necessary for survival, he did much to make life better for the people who had the good fortune to live alongside him.

Though Kit delighted in my ambition, he never failed to offer a bit of advice. After he retired, he'd often stop in for a cup of milky tea, and if I was flapping my hands in annoyance about some political issue, he'd say, 'Sometimes, Martin, you need to remember that your breath is for cooling your porridge with, and those hands are for blessing yourself!'

And then there is Dermot Mooney. Celtic-mad Dermot. Not just a stalwart volunteer and the man who organised that life-changing visit from Billy McNeill's team, but the person who saw us for who we were.

I remember about five years ago, I was in Newry, picking up a part for my adapted van, when I stopped at a little café. The only wheelchair access was through an adjoining second-hand bookshop, and as I was leaving, I picked up a couple of books from a display table, including a book on the history of soccer in Ireland. Three evenings later, the doorbell rang at home, and when I buzzed open the door, Dermot was standing there. He was suffering from Alzheimer's in his old age and seemed confused. He had strayed from his house, walking a couple of kilometres from Sutton to my cottage. But within minutes, he'd spotted the soccer book on my coffee table and picked it up. He sat down with it in his hand and started talking perfectly lucidly about the old days in Baldoyle. The hours flew by as we talked, until I realised I ought to ring his family, who turned out to

Never Know Your Place

be beside themselves with worry.

Dermot died three days later. I can't help thinking he made that last pilgrimage to Baldoyle because, though he was the one doing all the giving, his involvement in Baldoyle Hospital meant as much to him as it did to us.

Barbara and I remember Kit and Dermot's warm or positive words as chinks of light in a gloomy period, and our experience of institutional life gives us a particular unspoken bond. We were harshly separated the moment we arrived in Baldoyle, but we were together for the things that mattered most: the visits, the treats, the journeys, the holidays. We were among many thousands of Irish children to grow up in institutions in the mid-twentieth century. Back then, Irish society, and the Catholic Church in particular, had a 'special' place for any child who didn't fit the norm – whether that was because of disability or some other accident of their birth. It's important to remember what it felt like to be hidden away by that narrow and unkind world, so we don't make those mistakes again.

I wish I could say for certain that institutionalisation was a thing of the past, and that the right to PA services could be taken for granted, but budgets are being cut regularly, or tweaked off radar, and there are huge regional inequalities. An increasing number of young disabled people are not being allocated enough PA hours to enjoy the kind of freedom I have had.

This is not in the spirit of Independent Living that my generation fought so hard for.

Before I hang up my cap, I hope to see the next generation of Irish activists coming together to protect the PA service and to envision what a better future might look like for disabled people in Ireland.

My life has shown me that the people who change things the most are those who first find ways of changing how they see themselves. So, my

Epilogue

advice is this: Do everything you can to free your imagination. If you see a closed door, push it open. Stick your foot in there so others can follow you. If anyone suggests you are aiming too high, if anyone tries to tell you, explicitly or subtly, where you belong in the world, never listen. If there's one thing I know for certain, it's that you should never know your place.

Martin Naughton, 16 March 1954–13 October 2016

Afterword

Niall Ó Baoill

I have – almost without knowing it – always had a proprietorial interest in the life of Martin Naughton. Martin and I both arrived in the northside Dublin village of Baldoyle in the early 1960s – he from the west of Ireland and me from New York – and though it took several years for our paths to cross, as young people we shared a feeling of displacement, a sense of being personally and culturally restricted, and a desire to feel less dislocated from the people who lived their lives alongside us.

Martin tells his side of it vividly in the early chapters of this book. I, on the other hand, was one of the young children he describes as being released from 'high babies' in the national school at half three, genuflecting in front of the Church, and sprinting across the road to the railings of the 'Little Willie Hospital'. I remember standing there and beholding the curious young faces of the hospital children, with their wheelchairs, callipers, crutches or iron beds. Occasionally, some of the more mobile or curious hospital children might venture close to the railings, through which a piece of chewing gum or a kind word might elicit a brief response.

As 'children on the outside' we had so many questions about these 'children on the inside' but there was a lot that could not be easily said and so,

Afterword

sadly, we co-existed in a community without any direct relationship. That is until Martin made it his personal crusade to change this apartheid-like mentality and to open all our lives up to the possibilities of a more inclusive way of seeing the world.

As Martin describes in this book, our friendship kicked off when developing Baldoyle Hospital Sports Club (BHSC) with other De La Salle students. Much of the time we were working hard, and it was fascinating to witness how Martin set about animating people to his will and way of looking at things, ever widening his circle of influence and impact.

We worked together not just in BHSC but on broader community projects such as the integrated Youth Centre in Baldoyle, and over the years I saw how Martin was prepared to use every tool at his disposal – including the awkwardness of others around disability – to further his political aims. No exaggeration, he could make Government Ministers totter after him as though children in a trance. Once at a funeral wake, I watched Martin deliberately run his wheelchair onto the foot of the leader of Fianna Fáil, who being too polite to bring it to his attention, suffered in silence while Martin continued to make his point.

Politically, Martin could be a bull, but he was not a ruthless man. He had a large well of compassion and maintained a fierce loyalty to those who supported him. He also had a very respectful and considered way of checking in with people. It felt as though nothing essential was ever forgotten.

In later decades, we had a fixed arrangement to spend St Stephen's Day together and it was on that day in 2015, in the small sitting room of his cottage in Baldoyle, that Martin told me he had begun working with Joanna Marsden on this memoir.

Even reading an early draft, I recognised most everything about how he chose to express his experiences of family, childhood and the bitter loneliness of institutionalisation – and I found it all very moving and true. The text accurately chartered the many ventures leading up to his hard-got personal emancipation and his early efforts at living in the community. It was also on point concerning Martin's radicalisation around disability rights and the Independent Living movement, accurate in how it chartered his ingenuity and tireless endeavour to make a life for himself – despite the extreme odds – and how he blazed the trail for Independent Living in Ireland.

He had written a little about the later decades of his life, but those pages were much thinner and the focus of the memoir was clearly the trajectory of the first four decades of his life – from his early childhood in Spiddal up to 1995, the year in which he and his fellow activists finally convinced the Irish Government to fund Personal Assistant services.

Though the final two decades of his life are not the subject of this book, it is important to say that Martin did go on to achieve a great deal. For many years, he drove around Ireland week after week supporting disabled people who were setting up Centers for Independent Living in their regions. He helped grow Vantastic, the accessible transport service he and other activists set up in 1995 to plug the appalling gap in public transport. Working with fellow activists Donal Toolan, Selina Bonnie and Gordana Rajkov, he created a pioneering work exchange that trained PAs to work with disabled people in Ireland and Serbia. He founded 'Disability Options' to provide peer training in Independent Living, and Áiseanna Tacaíochta to encourage disabled people to manage their PA services through a 'Direct Payments' model. He was also a founder member of the European Network on Independent Living and established the internationally

Afterword

important 'Freedom Drive', a political march that takes place every two years in Brussels, with the aim of keeping Independent Living on Government agendas.

Martin liked to keep moving. He never sought a job in a service-providing organisation – the sort of a place where a person might become stuck in their ways – but he did establish a very flexible working relationship with the Disability Federation of Ireland where an open collegiality worked to good effect.

I spent a lot of time with him in his final two years and it was clear that revisiting his past through this memoir had re-awoken in him a sense of urgency about the future. Rather than finish the book, he became absorbed in activism again, laying the groundwork for a 'DPO' (a Disabled Persons' Organisation, to be run only by disabled people); organising a 'National Assembly' in Athlone with the aim of uniting people with physical, intellectual and mental disabilities; staging gruelling public protests against threatened cuts in State funding for PA services, highlighting the Government's tardiness in ratifying the United Nations Convention on the Rights for People with Disabilities (UNCRPD).

In March 2015, I accompanied Martin on a very personal pilgrimage along the Selma to Montgomery Heritage Trail in Alabama – 2015 being the fiftieth anniversary of this turning point regarding votes for black Americans, and also the twentieth anniversary of the passing of the Americans with Disabilities Act. Having long drawn inspiration from the American civil rights movement, Martin wanted to honour Martin Luther King and his fellow campaigners, and to remind himself of the power of action taken by people for themselves in the quest for liberty and equality.

It turned out to be a difficult journey, the Heritage Trail being in reality

Never Know Your Place

nothing more than a series of lonely metal notices, signposting the original resting points and campsites, at intervals along what is now a four-lane highway with no footpath. But Martin was not going to be put off by this, or by the hot and humid weather, the gigantic commercial trucks blasting their klaxons in disapproval, or the endless detritus on the road. One of Martin's colleagues, Orlaith Grehan, and I accompanied him, walking at a respectable distance behind to give him his personal space, and as one

Martin Naughton makes his way towards the Alabama State Capitol building, on the final leg of the Selma to Montgomery Heritage Trail in 2015, a personal pilgrimage to mark the fiftieth anniversary of this turning point regarding votes for black Americans.

Afterword

day turned to another, we witnessed his singular determination as he put in the hard miles on the often steeply inclined hard shoulder. It seemed to me that on that pilgrimage, Martin was not only paying tribute to his civil rights heroes, he was consciously giving himself the time to reflect on the people who had passed through his life – many of whom feature in his memoir.

Once the deeply personal journey was complete, Martin, with typical pragmatism, switched into political mode and, at the invitation of his old friend Judy Heumann, travelled to the State Department in Washington DC, where he gave American activists a history of the Independent Living movement in Ireland, before going off-script and regaling them with his memories of Fred Fay and Ed Roberts.

Martin reuniting with his old friend Judy Heumann in the Ralph J Bunche Library at the Department of State in Washington DC in 2015.

Never Know Your Place

In March 2016, Martin was made an Honorary Professor at the Centre for Disability Law and Policy in NUIG (now University of Galway). He accepted the award with slight embarrassment, conscious of his patchy education, but on the drive home from Galway he couldn't resist ringing Barbara to tease her, 'I'm a professor now, don't you know!'

But the exertion of Martin's US journey, together with the intensity of his renewed political activism, had taken its toll, and his health started to falter, resulting in his admission to Beaumont Hospital that autumn.

On Thursday 13 October 2016, Martin died. It shouldn't have been a shock, but it was for Barbara and the rest of Martin's family and countless friends. At his funeral in Baldoyle Church, it was clear from the crowded pews, and rows of wheelchair users in the aisles, that Martin had been many things to many people: an institutional survivor, a community leader, a battler against injustice and a visionary; a close friend, brother, uncle and indeed father figure/mentor.

Friend and fellow campaigner Donal Toolan gave the eulogy, and the sombre silence was broken by loud, uncontrollable laughter when Donal reminded mourners of three 'rules' by which Martin had lived his life:

1. If it is a good enough idea, someone will pay for it.
2. If it's not in writing, it never happened.
3. It's easier to get forgiveness than permission.

'The Sound of Silence' was played as we left the church and many of us joined the cavalcade crossing the country to Spiddal in Connemara. There, like a tribal leader being received by his own, Martin's remains were lowered and immediately covered in by local men, shovelling the earth to the soft tones of kind words in his native tongue and the accompanying tears of those gathered on the high ground overlooking Galway Bay.

Afterword

Martin Naughton's burial in Spiddal. He was buried beside his sister Maureen.

The impact of Martin's death was significant not only for his loving family and friends, and for the people whose lives he impacted in literally every county, but also in the political domain, where he ranked among the country's foremost social activists, as tributes from the President, Taoiseach and other public figures attested.

The year after Martin's death, his sister Barbara took the portrait of Martin painted by his friend Mary Duffy down from its place above the fireplace in his tiny cottage and drove it to the Centre for Disability Law and Policy at the University of Galway. It seemed the most fitting place for the portrait to hang in perpetuity; a reminder to students of an indefatigable civil rights campaigner who had achieved considerable social change but still saw the need to call the next generation to action.

Now, hopefully, this book can take its place alongside the portrait: Martin speaking for himself, and doing his utmost to have the last word – 'An focal deireanach' – as he always did.

Never Know Your Place

The portrait of Martin painted by his friend, artist and activist Mary Duffy. Martin said this painting was one of the only images of himself he ever liked.

Co-author's Notes

This book is first and foremost a memoir, and not intended to serve as a definitive or exhaustive historical record. The events are as recalled by Martin Naughton, with some input from those closest to him. Scenes and dialogue have been recreated based on memories, and in a few instances, names and details have been changed to protect the privacy of others. The dates given and chronology of events are as remembered by Martin. They have been checked where feasible, but it was impossible to verify all aspects of the story, such as the unusual train route via the (rarely used) Phoenix Park Tunnel, described by Martin in Chapter One.

In a couple of cases, events are slightly out of sequence in the narrative, to reflect the way in which they were recalled by Martin. Memories from regular events, such as summers in Spiddal, likely merged in Martin's memory.

Readers should note that St Mary's Orthopaedic Hospital for Children, or 'Baldoyle Hospital' as Martin called it, is no longer run by the Sisters of Charity. It was passed to St Michael's House in 2009.

Martin's experience of Baldoyle Hospital, while difficult, was perhaps more positive than for many others, in that he found ways to grow within an oppressive system. This memoir does not reflect the experiences of all who were there, and it is also clear that the hospital and its staff changed significantly over the years.

Working on this book, Martin was conscious that with hindsight and the higher expectations of today, the US in the 1990s was not the utopia

Never Know Your Place

for disabled people he once considered it, but it was progressive at that time. 'Everything I saw was framed by how behind we were in Ireland,' he said.

There was not scope within the final chapter of this book to write about The Forum of People with Disabilities, an organisation which was founded in the early 1990s to further the legal rights of disabled people.

However, for those interested in the history of disability activism in Ireland, it is important to point out that Martin had huge respect for the work undertaken by the Forum and in particular by Donal Toolan, Jacqui Browne, Mary Duffy and Austin O'Carroll.

Mayo journalist Donal Toolan played a central role in the establishment of the Commission on the Status of People with Disabilities in 1993, and Martin felt the work undertaken by the Commission undoubtedly helped pave the way for the success of his 1995 PA funding campaign, as well for later legislation.

CIL (Center for Independent Living) Dublin operates today as Independent Living Movement Ireland (ILMI). Separate Centres for Independent Living also developed around the country, many of which were set up with the support of Martin and his colleagues.

Additional information provided by Martin in the process of writing this book, but not included in the final book, including a few reflections on his projects post-1995, will be given to an archive to be set up in the library at the University of Galway in his name.

The specific scope of this book means that there are many important people in Martin's life whose names are not included, in particular more recent colleagues, younger family members and later PAs (many of whom were like family to Martin).

Co-author's Notes

There were also other significant relationships in Martin's life, but he was conscious of respecting privacy, and chose only to include Mary Llewellyn, who was both his first serious relationship and a lifelong friend. Martin would wish those not mentioned in this memoir to know that it is not a diminishment of their value in his life.

Endnotes

1. Micheál Ó Bríain joined the Abbey Theatre in 1943, where he appeared in countless plays. Much later, he became known for several roles for RTÉ television, including playing Michael McDermott in 'Glenroe'.
2. Although they were told off for using the wrong door, it was probably the main door just a few years earlier because a family is shown using it in a promotional film called *Little Lame Boy*. This film, made in 1960 to support the huge fundraising campaign for the hospital, was directed by William Fasbender and narrated by Cyril Cusack and premiered at the Savoy Cinema.
3. When Nurse Jones retired many years later, Martin recalled that she asked to stay on in Baldoyle Hospital because she considered the place to be her home. He said it reminded him that 'life wasn't easy for many women who worked in the hospital and it wasn't just the children who had to live with disappointments'.
4. Another good friend of Martin's was Seamus Haughton, who he remembered as 'the biggest daredevil in the place'.
5. Martin mentioned many other people who supported him at that time, and they included Noel Bell, Emmet Ó Baoill, Dominic O'Brien, Cathal McGuire, Des Duggan, Ronan Hughes, Tom McHale, Oona Brett, Gillian Mooney, Amanda McHugh, Sinead Maloney and Ann Sullivan.
6. Martin's business partner was Liam Leiden, and the company was called LEO (Leiden Employment Organisation).

Never Know Your Place

7   Regular members of the new group included Michael McCabe, Declan O'Keeffe, Peter Moore, Denis O'Brien, Dolores Murphy, Catherine Hickey, Dermot Walsh, Hubert McCormack and Ursula Hegarty. Several board members of the Irish Wheelchair Association, such as Jim Molloy, Brian Malone, Colm O'Doherty, Jim Dukes, and Jack Kerrigan, were also supportive. Not all of those involved in the early discussions went on to become official founders: Denis O'Brien died before CIL was formally founded; and Dolores Murphy, who did not have a disability but was a committed supporter of the principles of Independent Living, remained an employee of IWA.

8   Judy's life is documented in her memoir *Being Heumann: An Unrepentant Memoir of a Disability Rights Activist*, co-authored by Kristen Joiner. The memoir is currently being adapted into a movie. Judy is also featured in the Oscar-nominated documentary, *Crip Camp: A Disability Revolution* (Netflix).

9   The dialogue that follows was recorded by the manager of Operation Get-Out, Gordana Rajkov, and included in her memoir *Gordana Rajkov: Vying for a Choice*.

10 Christian O'Reilly went on to write *Inside I'm Dancing*, based on his experiences in those years, and also *No Magic Pill*, a play based on Martin Naughton's life. Other important contributors to CIL's daily work mentioned by Martin were Gráinne McGettrick, Noreen Halligan, Emma Flinter and law student Frederick Olulay.

11 Other protesters are believed to have included: Arron Abbey (RIP), James Brosnan (RIP), Eugene Callan (RIP), Eileen Daly, Florence Dougall (RIP), Ann Marie Flanagan, Dermot Hayes, Michael Keegan (RIP), Myles Kelly, Brian Malone (RIP), Michael McCabe, Peter

Endnotes

Moore, Joe T Mooney (RIP), Ciaran Nesbitt, Declan O'Keeffe (RIP), Gordon Ryan, Donal Toolan (RIP), and Dermot Walsh (RIP).

12 According to activist Selina Bonnie, Martin didn't like to use the word 'protest' and preferred the word 'action' because it was about 'seeking solutions rather than just complaining about things'.

13 Gerard Quinn went on to hold various influential posts, including professor of law at NUI Galway (now University of Galway), Ireland, and Director of the university's Centre for Disability Law and Policy. In October 2020, Quinn was appointed by the United Nations Human Rights Council as the UN Special Rapporteur on the Rights of Persons with Disabilities.

Acknowledgements

The long project to complete and oversee the publication of this book has been supported by the Disability Federation of Ireland (DFI), Irish Wheelchair Association (IWA), Independent Living Movement of Ireland (ILMI) and Michael Dawson. Particular thanks is due to Allen Dunne, for co-ordinating this support with warmth and enthusiasm and also being a thoughtful reader; Selina Bonnie, for brilliant contacts and guidance on language; Michael Doyle, for encouragement and advice; and Michael McCabe, for providing information and helpful suggestions.

This manuscript was completed with the help of Martin's sister, Barbara Naughton, his niece Nora Ann Naughton, and his many friends, former colleagues and PAs.

A particular debt is owed to Niall Ó Baoill, who gave a huge amount of time and energy to this project, including writing the Afterword and contributing several anecdotes to Martin's story; and to Rosaleen McDonagh for her very personal Foreword.

Thanks is also due to Mary Llewellyn, whose willingness to allow Martin to share details of their relationship added wonderful insights to this book.

Valuable input on the text and photos was provided by Nina Byrne, Emma Caparangca, James Cawley, Martin Costello, John Dolan, John Duffy, Sarah Fitzgerald, Dave Fitzgibbon, Eoin Healy, Michael Fleming, Vanessa Fox O'Loughlin, Damien Lynch, Judy Heumann (RIP), Mairéad Manton (RIP), Robby Martin, Hubert McCormack (RIP), John McDonald, Christy Moore, Brian Murphy, Sang Nguyen, Susan O'Brien,

Never Know Your Place

Brendan O'Connor, Christian O'Reilly, Ching Pang, Gordana Rajkov (RIP), Teresa Ranson, Kathleen Reynolds, Natasha Spremo, Mary Stanley, Damien Walshe and Aisling Whelan.

Essential guidance was given by Mladen Tubic, Kieran Loughran and Matthew Austin, and encouragement and practical support, before and after Martin's death, came from those listed above and also from Cuong Bui, Padraig Cormican, Hung Da, Sinisa Kasalovic, Des Kenny, Ned McLoughlin, Marco Parisi, Dragana Pekez, Bozo Sicar, Sinisa Sicar, Branco Spremo, Colin Wright, and all of Martin's PAs.

Assistance was given in the checking of facts and the sourcing of a number of archive photos by local historian Michael J Hurley; Amy Bramley at Dublin Bus; transport experts Cyril McIntyre, Oliver Doyle and Ciarán Cooney (the IRR Archive); *The Irish Times*; Bruce Fay, Derick Fay and Trish Irons; Mairéad Delaney and Stephen Maloney at the Abbey Theatre; and Alexis Dobbin and the great John Fallon (aka the 'thirteenth Lion')' at Celtic Football Club.

Huge thanks is due to editor Susan Houlden for her warm professionalism, sound guidance and unfailing enthusiasm for the story; to Kunak McGann and Kasandra Ferguson for believing in the book from the beginning; and to designer Emma Byrne and all the team at the O'Brien Press.

A personal thank you from Joanna goes to Brian Dunphy, Samuel Marsden Dunphy and Petros Marsden Dunphy for their patient support throughout this project, and to Jennifer Marsden for reading the manuscript and taking an interest in Martin's story from the beginning.

Gratitude is also owed to Prof Eilionóir Flynn and Dr Barry Houlihan at the Centre for Disability Law and Policy in University of Galway, whose commitment to archiving Martin's photos and papers in the

Acknowledgements

library at University of Galway is a symbolic first step towards recording Irish disability history; to curator Iarlaith Ní Fheorais and the 2023 TULCA Festival of Visual Arts for including an excerpt from this book in their publication; and to Turlough O'Riordain and Eoin Kinsella, editors of Cambridge University Press's *Irish Dictionary of Bibliography*, whose inclusion of an entry on Martin in a forthcoming edition acknowledges Martin's role in the nation's history.

Lastly, there may well be many more names that Martin would have liked to have mentioned or thanked. This list was incomplete at the time of his death, so please forgive the inevitable omissions.

From a young age, Shane Carthy had an amazing talent for sport. He quickly rose up through the ranks of Dublin football, playing on an All Ireland-winning team at the age of eighteen. In the midst of all of this success, he increasingly suffered from severe bouts of depression, hiding this from all around him. For two long years, as he triumphed on the football field, he suffered through constant mental turmoil.

With searing honesty, he tells of his journey through deepest depression, leading him to become hospitalised at nineteen years old, and how he learned to overcome his troubles and to love life again.

> 'A story of perseverance, offering hope to anyone who suffers debilitating depression … Carthy writes with honesty and courage, capturing his frightening journey, which almost led to suicide.'
>
> *Irish Examiner*

Great books from
O'BRIEN
Hundreds of books for all occasions

From beautiful gifts to books you'll want to keep forever! The best writing, wonderful illustration and leading design. Discover books for readers of all ages.

Follow us for all the latest news and information, or go to our website to explore our full range of titles.

TheOBrienPress   TheOBrienPress
OBrienPress   TheOBrienPress

Visit, explore, buy
obrien.ie